Dedication

This book is dedicated to our dad and the many memories we had with him; and to our mom for always being there for us, and for all the fun times that we have had and that are still ahead for us all, together, on our paths of life.

Acknowledgments

Our first thanks go to Mom for being such a positive influence and for always being a pillar of strength and encouragement that we can lean on; thanks also to our family and friends for their constant support and love through the worst times and the best times; and thanks to the wonderful staff at Free Spirit, especially Judy and Ellen, for having faith in us and for believing in our message.

Contents

Introduction

This is a journal about what happened to us. We're three ordinary kids, with two great parents. Our mom is a lawyer and our dad is a doctor. Well, actually we should say he *was* a doctor. You see, we were a normal family one day, and then all of a sudden, everything changed. One night, Dad just died and that was that. He had an *arrhythmia*—that means his heart started beating in the wrong rhythm and couldn't correct itself. That made him die. It happened in the middle of the night, when he was sleeping. It's like there have been two parts to our lives— the time before Dad died and the time after he died.

Since you're reading this, then you probably know what we're talking about. Maybe you had someone close to you who died or know someone like that. Maybe you even lost both parents. It's the biggest bummer ever.

When our dad died, Mom got books from friends and from the library and stuff. They were a little helpful, but there were no books from a kid's point of view. When grown-ups tell you things, sometimes it's hard to understand because they don't always remember how it was to be a kid. No matter what we read, we couldn't believe that the bottomless pit in our hearts would ever go away. Because when it first happens, your whole world falls apart, and you really feel like it's the end. And sometimes you find yourself wishing that your life was over, too. To go on without the person who died seems too impossible.

Well anyway, that's how the three of us felt. We're pretty lucky because we've all always been close, so we talked about everything. But you know all the stuff the adults around you are saying? Things like, "Time will make it better," "Your dad would want you to go on living a happy life," and "You'll be happy again." It's hard to listen to adults who tell you that. What do they know? Most of them got to grow up with their parents. Well, the thing is that all that stuff they tell you—it's all pretty much true. Your life goes on, and of course it will never be close to the same. You can't expect it to go back to how it was.

It takes a lot of work on your part, and it takes time, too, but life does get good again if you let it. Only it gets good in a new way. Things are always changing. Nothing stays the same. You have a pet and then it may run away or die, or you change grades and make new friends. There are lots of different changes. Having someone die is a HUGE change, and not a good one, because you miss the person so much. But you learn to make your new life, and it's still great and there are fun times. Giggling attacks and all kinds of silly things still happen. And you learn to think about the person who died and feel happy.

Hey, it's not something that happens in a day, and it sure isn't easy. But it really happens if you give it a chance. The hole in your life mends itself and you can go on with a new, happy life. We were all SO close to Dad, and we thought he was the best dad in the whole wide world. And we still think that, even if he's not here anymore.

We want you to know that what's happened is manageable if you give yourself a chance to deal with all of the things that you're feeling now and will feel later. There are sad times and mad times and feeling guilty that maybe it was your fault times, and every other kind of time that you can imagine. But every kid feels all of those things in one way or another. It's normal. And if you let yourself feel those things and go through all that stuff, then you will be okay. It's the kids who act like nothing happened, or act like the world owes them everything and are always mad at everyone, who can't get past it all. You have to help yourself be strong and think positively and get through it. Because you can if you work at it. And it's worth it to work at it. Believe us, we know. We felt like we would never be happy again, and we really are. Sure, there are still times when one of us will start crying or just feel totally bummed out that Dad is gone, but then we cheer up.

Your thoughts and feelings about the person will always be with you, because it would be too sad to think that you could forget. But you can have that person with you in a happy way.

We didn't really have any kids to tell us that. That's why we're writing this book. Read all of it or just some parts here and there. Then in another few months, read it again, because things change in your head every few months and things that didn't make sense start to.

Well, anyway, here's our journal. We wrote a lot about the first week and the funeral and stuff, and you might have already dealt with that. Or maybe that's still coming. Being prepared is really helpful. Wherever you are in the process, it's the kind of stuff that keeps going through your head a million times. And it's important to have it straightened out to deal with everything that happened and that you felt, because that is the worst part.

We also included a part at the end of each section called "Looking Back," which tells thoughts we had as we reread our journals later on. We discuss what we think was good or bad about how things were handled, or how we handled ourselves. It might give you some ideas for yourself.

So anyway, we hope this helps you sort through your feelings and deal with things in a positive way.

Amy, David, and Allie

Amy (now 15), David (now 11), Allie (now 15)

Finding Out That Dad Died

Amy *(8 years old at the time):* When Mom woke us up in the middle of the night and said that Dad had died, I felt like I didn't really know what the word meant. I guess it was like too much to handle. So my brain didn't want to absorb it. I kept thinking that it wasn't really true. That maybe I was just having a really bad dream or something. Just before I went to bed, I had helped Dad figure out which outside lights weren't working. I kissed him goodnight and he said to have a great school day if he'd left for work before I was awake. And now he was dead. He couldn't be!

David *(4 years old at the time)*:* When Mom woke me up, I thought I heard her wrong. I didn't even really understand what she said. I was in the middle of a dream about a farm and I got mixed up. I thought she was talking about the pig on the farm dying. It almost seemed funny. But I saw my sisters crying and Mom crying and knew something bad was happening. Mom told me again what was going on. Then I was crying and feeling pretty sad. I didn't understand death as much as I do now, so mostly I was confused and sad to see everyone else upset. I didn't know how much of a forever thing death is.

Allie *(8 years old at the time, Amy's identical twin):* I woke up in the middle of the night to go to the bathroom.

---

* Because David was too young to write for himself, he dictated his sections to his mother. She typed them, but the words are his.

I heard my grandmother screaming and crying and I heard Mom saying something to her about Dad dying. It had to be a nightmare! Grandma doesn't live in our house, so how could she be there in the middle of the night? I hid my head in my pillow and I tried to go back to sleep. If only it was that easy to make something bad go away. A minute or two later, Mom came in and she told us what happened. Mom said maybe David wouldn't understand because he was only four years old. I felt grown-up when Amy and I helped explain it to him. Like, Dad just went to heaven, or Dad is visiting G—d* and won't be coming back, or he's on a trip, or something like that. I remember David woke up and made us laugh because he was sleep-talking. It's hard to believe that at that minute we actually laughed, but I guess it was all so weird. Then we got him up and Mom just told him.

There is no right way to hear about the death of one of your parents. Sometimes you might not find out right away because your parent or whoever is totally freaking out and they need some time to get themselves together before being able to talk to you. And there are calls that must be made, like to your grandparents, aunts and uncles, or other family and friends. So if you ever look back and feel mad about the way you found out, just drop it. It's the most awful time in everyone's life and you need to give your parent or other relatives a break.

*In the Jewish religion, the name of God is generally not spelled out fully, out of respect.

One big thing you learn is that everyone is having lots of mixed emotions and you all need to try to not be too hard on each other. Everyone handles tough things in their own way, so you need to respect that. If it's something that really bothers you, you should discuss it, but then you need to drop it and move on. Some things can't be changed once they're done. So if you're sad or mad about the way you were told about your parent's death, tell your parent, or whoever told you, how you feel. Then really listen to what they have to say. After you've all said your feelings, you need to respect their decisions and move past it.

The Night He Died

Amy: Every once in a while, someone came into our bedroom where we were hanging out with Mom the whole night. Our grandparents and some cousins kept telling us that it was going to be okay, and stroking our hair and stuff. I didn't like that. Nothing would ever be okay again—Dad was dead! And they were kind of staring at us when they thought that we couldn't see them. But you know how you can always feel when someone is staring at you? I wanted to be left alone and wanted them to go away. They pretty much did, because none of us were talking to them too much. They probably wanted to talk to Mom, but she wouldn't leave us in the room alone. Mom would tell each one that we needed our space and they went back out to the den.

I remember that Mom kept telling us that we might not want to go out of our room because there were so many police and other people around in the house. One time, two or three policemen came into our room to give us Dad's jewelry, like his watch and wedding ring. I felt like I stopped breathing for a minute to see Dad's stuff in Mom's hand, not on Dad. It was all too weird and awful to really be happening.

They also came in later to ask if anyone wanted to see Dad's dead body before they took it away. I guess they were getting ready to load it into the ambulance. We all three wanted to pretty bad, because that would be the last time to give him a hug or kiss, but Mom said no. When I asked her why not, she said because that would be the last thing that we would remember and we would always have that in our minds. She said he wasn't Dad anymore, it was just his skin and not his soul by then. I kind of wished that I had seen him because I thought it was important to say good-bye. But now I understand more about the soul and body being different and I know what she meant. Mom said she couldn't get that picture of him being dead out of her head for a really long time. So I'm glad now that we didn't see him like that.

Allie: None of us really remember too much about that night. We decided that in a couple of years we might ask our grandparents to fill in the details of what actually happened in the rest of the house that night.

Mom told us that she thought Dad died from a heart attack. Mom woke up in the middle of the night and Dad had fallen asleep lying in bed with the TV on. She tried to wake him up to tell him to turn it off and he didn't wake up. So she had to call 911 and they told her he was dead. She said they couldn't be sure what it was until they did some tests. It was too hard right then to bother trying to understand how a healthy heart could have an attack.

When I think of the beginning, I guess I didn't really even understand that Dad was dead all that well. Or maybe I was purposely not understanding, hoping that maybe it would all just go away. For example, Amy and I had planned a special field trip with a lower-grade class. We had organized a beach cleanup for their class and our teachers were letting us go as special guests. I asked Mom if we could still go. Dad had died a few hours ago, and I was ready to go on a field trip?! That's pretty weird now that I think back about it. I guess I really was denying that the whole thing was happening. Of course, we didn't go on the trip, and by the time the morning came around it seemed more real that Dad was dead and I didn't want to go anyway.

Later, I felt guilty for even thinking about still going on the field trip. Sometimes you think things that don't make any sense. It doesn't mean you're a bad person. I guess for that moment I wanted everything to just be the same as it had been. Even if we'd gone on the field trip, of course, it wouldn't ever have been the same, but it was a normal reaction to a situation that was too much to deal with.

David: It was weird that there were so many people in our house in the middle of the night. I'm glad we had our own space, because there were a lot of relatives and friends around all the time. Lots of people flew in for the funeral. It was a pain, especially because we weren't that much into playing. I tried to think about what it would be like to grow up without Dad. It freaked me out—I couldn't even imagine it.

LOOKING BACK

This is a really tense time and no one really knows what to do. It's important to let your parent or relative or someone close to you know what you'd like or need. For instance, you might want to hang out with your parent, a grandparent, or a friend or someone. You'll need someone to listen to you, because your head will be spinning with a million thoughts, most of them sad. And you may have to choose someone besides a parent to talk to if your parent is busy with arrangements, or just too out of it, or if you lost both your parents. Since kids don't usually understand too much about death, it's important to ask questions. The more you ask, the better you'll understand. Death is the ending to life, just like being born is the beginning. It's just one of the stages, but it's the saddest stage so it's really hard.

And even though it's hard, you have to accept your parent's or relative's decisions on some of the big things. Like about looking at the dead body. Even if they make the wrong decision, they're just trying to do what they think is best for you. In the end, we're really happier that we didn't see his body. We're glad to remember him alive and happy.

Mom & David, 3/96

The Day Before the Funeral

Allie: Dad died in the middle of the night on Valentine's Day. By the morning, Dad's cousin had set up a table with a lot of food and a huge pot of coffee. A lot of Mom and Dad's friends had started to come over. They said they'd heard Dad died and couldn't believe it. We came out of the room and everyone was weird and freaked out when they saw us. Even though we're just kids, we could tell right away how uncomfortable they were. They tried to smile at us and kept saying that it would be all right. But we knew that it wouldn't be because Dad was dead. It was so dumb and annoying to keep hearing that, and especially to see all the fake smiles they put on in front of us. Did they think we didn't know they had been crying? It would have been better if they'd acted around us how they felt—sad. But no one did. I guess they didn't know what to say, but it made me feel a lot worse. It was weird to see so many grown-ups crying.

We were all kind of mad at Mom that she was letting these people come over. We wanted to just keep the door locked and put a sign on the front door to please leave us alone. But she said that they were sad, too, and that it was a natural thing for friends to come together to share their sadness. I guess I understand, but we gave her a pretty hard time about it. At least she hung out with us a lot, so that was good. I didn't want to be alone, but I didn't want anyone but her and David and Amy.

Later that day, Grandpa (we call him Zayde, which is a Jewish term for grandpa) and Mom had to go to the funeral place and make the plans. That was the first time that Mom left our side since it happened, but our grandparents were there and they basically left us alone, like we wanted. They'd check up on us now and then, but Mom had asked them to let us be by ourselves unless we wanted something. It was all so confusing and so much to think through. It's the kind of thing we didn't want to talk about at the beginning with anyone except our immediate family. We're lucky because we're really close to all of our grandparents, but we're even closer to Mom and wanted to handle it with her. And our grandparents were sad for having their son die, but our sadness was for a different relationship being gone, our dad. They had their sorrow to deal with and we had ours.

I wasn't even sure what a funeral really was. I knew it was something with a coffin being buried under the ground. It seemed pretty simple, and on the cartoons it didn't seem so hard and hurtful. Real life is very different. Mom sat down with us and explained exactly what it would be like. I didn't realize that there would be speeches and all kinds of other parts, too.

Mom let us pick out a few drawings each to put in Dad's coffin. It was hard to choose what would be with him forever. Suddenly, nothing was good enough. And then, the good stuff we all kind of wanted to save because it was the last stuff we ever made for him.

David: My sisters and I played and did crafts by ourselves when Mom went to make plans for the funeral. My grandmothers kept coming in to check on us. They just wanted to help, but we wanted to be on our own. They were just crying the whole time and it was kind of annoying because then we would start crying, too. And they couldn't comfort us the way Mom could. And even Mom wasn't that good at it. Because there isn't too much anyone can say that will help you deal with the fact that your dad is dead.

David's drawing of playing in the pool with Dad

We needed to get some stuff to give the funeral guy for Dad. Mom had told us to either draw a picture or get an old one to put in Dad's coffin. Every time I'd find a picture, I kind of didn't want to give it to Dad because then I wouldn't ever see that again either. All our aunts and uncles flew in from all over the country the day before the funeral. I was excited to see them. It was sad to see Mom and her sisters all hugging and crying because they're always hugging and laughing. That gave me a pretty bad stomachache. But by the end of that day, I was used to seeing adults crying. Which is weird.

A lot of the time, I made myself think about something else, because it was too hard to deal with the forever part of it.

Amy: By the time the morning came, we weren't crying that hard. We'd all slept a little bit, and David was still asleep because he was so little and really tired. Allie and I were playing cards and we were doing okay. We mostly stayed in our playroom, so we were on our own. But when anyone came in and said anything to us about it, we both started crying pretty hard.

Mom and Dad's friends and our aunts and uncles were all being friendly and acting nice to each other. They talked about where they were from, what their job was, that kind of polite stuff. That was so dumb, because everyone had a broken heart and they weren't really into laughing at each other's dumb jokes when Dad's dying was on their minds. Why do grown-ups do so much fake stuff? They all were pretending to be happy. I felt like screaming at them to wipe the smiles off their faces. They were there because Dad was dead. What was there to smile about?

Their laughing and conversations were annoying, but when I saw someone crying, I kind of felt like, *What are YOU crying about? He was MY father.*

Mom came back from the funeral place and said the funeral would be the next day. She said we needed to pick out what Dad would be buried in. His dad wanted him to wear his best clothes, a suit and tie. Mom said his best clothes were the ones we had made him. I was pretty mad at my grandfather because he didn't live with Dad, so why should he choose what he would wear? But then he said, "Well, all right, whatever you think is best." We chose Dad's camping hat, his lucky argyle socks, two shirts that we had painted, and his best jeans. Dad would have been happy with that. It was obvious that his dad wasn't really happy with our decision, but at least he didn't make a fight out of it. He's usually pretty mellow about that kind of thing. And it was pretty important to us that Dad be comfortable.

LOOKING BACK

The thing is, a lot of adults don't really understand death and can't deal with it either. So you need to give them a break because they're freaked out to lose a friend, and then on top of that they see the person's kids and feel really sad for you. They all act awkward because it's a new experience for them and they're not sure what to do and how to be. If they cry, then you're like, *What are* you *crying about?* And if they smile, then you feel like, *Wipe that smile off your face!* So they can't really win. It's important to remember that and not throw a fit. And it's weird to see adults crying, because kids aren't used to that. It's almost a little scary. Sometimes it's best to just get your own space, in your playroom or bedroom. Put a sign on the door that says, "Please leave us alone," and then do your own thing. Have a relative or someone in there with you if you want.

You might feel angry about some of the things that happen, like when everyone invaded our space and came to the house that day. But that's what people do, and there's no stopping it. Even Mom didn't really want everyone there while she was still totally freaking out. But she handled it because you have to give everyone else a place to come and grieve together. Those kinds of things are not worth getting upset about, because however you feel they're still going to happen. That's how it's done when someone dies, and just because you don't like it doesn't mean that it's going to change. There are a lot of people involved—relatives, friends, coworkers. It's something that you just need to compromise on and find a place where you can be left alone if that's what you want.

There are a lot of rules and requirements that have to be followed, so you need to just accept those. But there are some things that the adults can compromise on and let you help with, and it's great when you can. Like it was great that we got to be part of the decision about what Dad was going to wear. And putting pictures or photos in the coffin is a good way to feel like a part of it. Or you might want to write a letter to go in the coffin, if you can. It's good to discuss things as they're happening with your parent or whoever, so you can all try to participate.

The Funeral

Allie: Mom had explained the different parts of the funeral to us so we'd know what to expect. She said all the grown-ups would be crying and that it would be kind of weird and scary-ish to see. I'm glad Mom warned us, because it was pretty strange. I mean, after two days we were getting used to seeing the grown-ups cry, but at the funeral they were crying really hard and making moaning and sobbing noises and everything. Sometimes we'd look at each other when someone blew their nose really loud, but none of us felt like laughing the way we usually would.

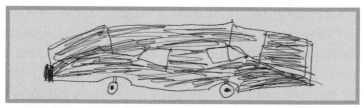

We all got to ride in black limos. When they pulled up to the house that morning, the three of us were secretly excited to ride in them, because we had never ridden in a limousine before. It was so big, and David was testing out all of the buttons. It was kind of cool and made me forget some of the nervousness. Mom didn't want to get in, but everyone was already loaded in and waiting. Finally, one of her sisters went in and walked her out and she got in. I felt bad for her because she was feeling and looking pretty bad. She didn't even wear mascara or comb her hair. So then we thought about where we were going and it wasn't so exciting anymore. Luckily, our aunts talked a lot and told funny stories during the ride, so it kept our minds off of where we were headed. After everyone had gone through about one box of tissues, we were there, at the funeral home.

I was nervous because I wasn't sure what the funeral would really be like. There were so many people all over the place. We were sent into a small, private room at the funeral place. We started with a short cere- mony where the rabbi tore black ribbons and pinned them over our hearts. I think it was a symbol to show how our hearts were ripped apart, just like the ribbon. A lot of people came up to us, like people did at the house. They asked us how we were and talked about stupid things. They were like conversations when you run into a friend at a store. Not one person said, "I know you must be really sad," or "This funeral is pretty tough." I would have appreciated their honesty.

The funeral guy led all of Dad's family into the front of the big room where the service was. As we walked in, I heard people whispering that we were his kids. It got really quiet before we even sat down. I looked around as we were led to our seats and it was jammed—there were people in every seat, standing in the back, all around the aisles, even in the outside halls. We were told later that there were so many people that they set up a speaker in the parking lot so everyone could hear the service. We each held Mom's hands (even though there were three of us and only two hands—we all squeezed together), and we walked right to the front row. That made me feel really important. Since Dad was a really good doctor, a lot of his patients and other doctors came. It made me feel proud that so many people knew Dad. I wished he was around so I could have told him how proud I was.

Amy: Mom said to wear whatever we wanted for the funeral.
Allie and I chose the dresses we
wore when we went out with Dad
on a date. David wore his "Dad
clothes"—you know, button-down
shirt and pants. Mom wore a black
dress because she said that most adults
wear black to a funeral. When she got home from the
funeral, she took it off and just threw it in the garbage!

The funeral service was very weird, because Dad was
right there in the front, in the wooden coffin. The cover
was closed, but to know that he was right in there was
an impossible thought. There was a service, and then
Dad's brother and sister both spoke about Dad. I felt bad
for Dad that Mom didn't give a speech for him because
he would have wanted her to do that. But she was crying too much and had Dad's sister say something on our
behalf. It was hard to pay attention because I was crying so much, not believing what was going on. Every
once in a while, I snuck a peek behind us, because we
were in the front row. Sometimes I saw someone waving
at me, but I never waved back.

At the end of the service, the guy was telling us to
walk with him to the limousines. We went up to the coffin and rubbed our hands on it. I wanted to open it up
and jump right in and give Dad the biggest, tightest hug
ever. But I knew that even though I was so close to him,
he was still impossibly far away and that I couldn't do
that. Ever again.

Of course, all that crying made me have to go to the
bathroom and we went before we got in the limousine.
The funeral guy was kind of annoyed with Mom about

that, but she didn't really care. There was a long line at the bathroom, but we went right to the front. (That was kind of cool.) I heard all the old ladies whispering about us, and some of them stroked our heads and stuff. But we ignored them because we were all freaked out at that point and getting fed up with all the strangers and stuff.

David: It was hard to believe that Dad was in the coffin in the front of the chapel. The cover was closed so we couldn't see him. But I knew he was right there. I asked Mom if we could open it and just give him one last hug and kiss, but we couldn't. She said that his body didn't look the same without his soul, which was really the Dad part of him. His soul was already in heaven, and the body was empty and not Dad anymore. I wasn't sure about all that.

I wore a nice pair of pants and a jacket to the funeral. I felt like I looked like Dad and that he would have been proud of me. I wasn't even that sad on the ride in the limo to the funeral, because I got so busy trying all the window and door buttons, and there were so many lights! At the cemetery, we sat in the front row again. This time, there were only a few chairs and most people had to stand. So that was pretty important. But I kind of wished I was someone not important and that the whole thing wasn't about someone in my family. At the end of the prayers, we all used a special shovel and one at a time we got some dirt and threw it on the coffin. Mom fainted for a minute because she was so sad and had been crying so much. I was pretty scared that she might have to hold onto someone else for the rest of that time. Then it wouldn't be just us four hanging onto each other there.

It's really helpful to have someone explain exactly what to expect for all the different parts of the funeral. You might have the coffin open and see the dead body or you might need to say something or walk to a certain place. It makes it easier to know what will happen and all the different steps because then you aren't so nervous about it.

Since it's your parent, it's important to be a part of the ceremony if you can. For instance, you might want to have someone say something in their funeral speech for you. Or have a certain song played. We were lucky that Dad's family and Mom let us help make the decisions. They were pretty good about compromising on some of the things that we'd decided. It may not be that way in your family, and they may be more strict about how things will be. If that happens, then say what you want in your head while the speeches are going on. Your parent will get the message just the same.

You might want to decide ahead of time who you'll hang out with at the funeral. We sat next to Mom, but sometimes it may not work out that way, and it would be good if you can figure out ahead of time who to sit next to.

Lots of times, the kids don't even go to the funeral. They're too young to understand it and may not be able to behave during it. It's probably a good idea to go if you can behave, because after all, it is your parent. Even if you don't understand what's going on, you can quietly make up your own prayer or something. But if you end up being left home during the funeral, oh well—it's still the same prayer in your head, whether it's

during the funeral service or months later and somewhere else. Your parent or whoever made a decision
that maybe it would be too tough for you to be there—
or whatever. They don't have a lot of practice in this
area, and probably neither does anyone else they can
talk to. So if you feel that they were wrong and you
should have been there, then just tell them. But then it's
over. There's no point in being really angry or throwing
a big dumb fit about it because there's nothing that can
change it now anyway.

Some people don't even have funerals. They have a
memorial, or a cremation, or something else. Everyone
does it their own way, because everyone has their own
religious rules or spiritual ideas. If you wanted it to be a
different way, imagine it in your mind or write it down.
In the end, it's the same thing as long as one way or
another you deal with the fact that the person is dead.

And it's important to think about
stuff like bringing a snack, going
to the bathroom at the right
time, those things. You might
have to suggest it to an adult
since they probably aren't
thinking about those kinds of
things with all the other stuff
that's going on. But it can be
pretty important, and it's better to
plan those things out in advance. Like if
we hadn't gone to the bathroom at the funeral home,
we would have had a big problem. There's no bathroom anywhere around at the cemetery, and not even
any trees to hide behind in an emergency. So it was a
good thing we went to the bathroom when we did.

After the Funeral

Amy: After the service at the cemetery was over, we took our last ride in the limo to the house. Part of our rock collection was in a bowl by the front door because we had wanted Dad to get some spiders out of it. People thought that it was a symbolic thing and picked a rock out of the bowl and held it for a couple seconds. Ew!!

After the funeral, people usually come back to the dead person's house for food. And they keep stopping by with meals and snacks. In a Jewish home, like ours, this lasts for between three to seven days and is called the *shiva*. It felt like our house was being invaded, because most of the people from the funeral came right over. I mean, it was everyone we knew and even more people we didn't know. There was brown paper over all of the mirrors because mourners aren't supposed to worry about how bad they look. Later on, my friends and I drew on the paper with crayons and markers. My friends were more into it than I was, because for them it was just a huge, fun drawing place. I kept thinking that the paper was there because Dad died, and it wasn't so much fun.

One of my friends asked, "Hey Amy, why aren't you crying? I thought you would be." That got me SO upset. She only came over for a little while, and I had good times and bad times that day. She happened to come during one of the good times. I thought, *What do you expect, that I'm going to cry every minute for the rest of my life?* But the truth is, I felt guilty that I was having fun. Maybe I was supposed to be more sad. Then I calmed down and decided I would just feel how I felt and not worry if it was right or not. Mom said that Dad would have thought that was the right thing to do, and that he wouldn't want us to be any more sad than we had to be.

During the next couple of days, people continued to come over to our house and give us little gifts and stuff. During this time, Mom spent a lot of time listening to us and talking with us. We read some books about death and talked afterwards about how we felt.

David: I liked all of the food that came. There were tons of great cookies and candy and stuff. But there were so many people walking in and out of the house all the time that it was hard to get the food without being stopped. Then I'd have to talk to them, and I didn't even know them. Mom hardly even knew them, and she didn't talk to them too much either. She let our grandparents do the talking. She'd tell them that she didn't want to hear their stories about Dad because she was too sad, but they would just tell her stuff anyway. So she stopped talking to most of the people and she said it was easier for her.

Even though some people who came were Mom and Dad's friends who I knew, it got annoying. I wanted everyone to leave so we could get back to the way things were. Mom said that Dad's patients were coming to be nice, but Amy and Allie said they didn't feel like being nice back. So neither did I. We just wanted to be left alone. Sometimes my friends came over. It was fun to play with them, like old times.

One time, I was playing Wiffle ball in the backyard and one of my friends' dads was pitching. It was pretty fun, but then I started thinking, *My dad will never pitch.* So I put the bat down and went into the house. It wasn't fun anymore. That was a sad time for me.

I was kind of sad when I would think about the Dad thing, but sometimes I was kind of not. I mean, I didn't cry all the time, but the tears would come and go. Whenever I saw my sisters or my mom crying, then I would usually start because I missed Dad so much already. Amy and Allie and I hung around together the whole time. We even pushed two twin beds together and all slept there. I'm glad they're around because they take care of me.

Allie: Mom told us there were going to be a lot of people in the house, so if we wanted our own space we could just go in our room with the door closed. I'm glad she told us what to expect all the time because it made it easier to handle.

We weren't sure that we were going to want to see anyone back at the house. And since there were more than fifteen hundred people at his funeral and the roads were jammed up, you can imagine how many people came to our house after that. We started out in Mom's room with Mom because there were too many people and we were just in a sad mood and wanted to have our own space. Mom's sisters were at the bedroom door making sure that only a few people could come in—only Mom's close friends and family.

Then after a little while, we went out of the room for some lunch. I wanted Mom to come with us. We really hadn't been apart except when she had to make the funeral arrangements. But she said that she didn't want to leave her room because then she would have to talk to people, and she wasn't up to it. I was kind of frustrated about that, because I didn't really want to go out without her, and we needed to eat something. But Mom just said she couldn't handle seeing anyone, so she stayed in her room and we went out with Aunt Sue. And Mom looked so bad at this point, maybe it was better that not too many people saw her. A lot of people came over to us, but Aunt Sue kept us moving so they couldn't stop us for too long. I was trying to keep in the tears when everyone was saying "Hello" and "How are you?" and pretending it was a good day.

We had started to get a little silly because there were so many people and we were getting all the attention. You know how that is. We were laughing and joking around even though the adults were still crying. One of my uncles took us outside to play ball and we calmed down. That was weird because earlier we'd been crying with big broken hearts.

Our teachers came, and David's teachers from preschool were there, too. We were all pretty shy during those times because it's not normal to have your teacher in your house.

LOOKING BACK

During the time after the funeral, when you're home grieving, it's good to have some of your friends come by. You think at the beginning that it might be awkward and you won't feel like playing, but that's not really how it is. They come over and everyone feels weird for a few seconds while they say they're sad for you, and then you do feel like playing. And it's great because you actually have a little fun and can forget most of what's happened for a little while. It's nice to have that break from all the heavy sadness.

You shouldn't feel bad if your friends say dumb things. Think about it—if the grown-ups are saying all the wrong things, how hard is it for a kid to know what to say? You wouldn't know what to say if it was you visiting one of your friends in that situation. So don't make too much out of it if they say something that bothers you, because at least they're there and trying.

Also, you can't be too hard on yourself. It's important to remember that it's okay to be happy and have fun. At the beginning, we felt guilty for not crying the whole time. After all, we loved Dad so much and now he was dead. But you know what? He wouldn't really want us to be crying the whole time. Only cry when you feel like crying, and if you can find a reason to smile or laugh, do it! As long as you're dealing with your sad times and letting out the tears when you need to, then it's okay to let out the giggles when they come along, too.

David, Allie, and Amy
at Marco Beach, FL, 6/96

The First Week

Amy: Most Jewish people have a *shiva* for seven days, but we'd seen enough people and we'd had enough of the whole thing after three days. Dad's parents did it for the whole seven days, but we only did it for three. Mom said that Dad would want us to do what was best for us and that we'd gotten enough out of the three days already. Dad's father wasn't shaving, because that's something that Jewish men do for the first month. He looked all hairy on his face and sloppy. He's more careful about following the rules of the religion than we are—like wanting to have services every morning and every evening at the house for the whole week of the *shiva*. The services are when they say the special mourning prayers, and a certain number of grown-ups have to be there before the prayer can be held, so people stop by to help say them.

I could tell that Grandpa thought we should have the *shiva* at our house for the whole time, but he was nice about letting us do our own thing. I'm glad that he respected our decision.

Besides, we felt like we needed our own space to think things through. You know, like how we'd live and that kind of thing. It felt great to have our house back. We went to our grandparents' house a couple of times because Mom said that we should be there for them, but it was very upsetting. There were a lot of their old friends sitting around and everyone kind of whispered and stared at us with sad looks when we came in. We didn't stay too long, because it made us feel so heavy and sad again.

David: For a week, we didn't ever go to the grocery store or do errands, which was great. We'd all had enough of talking to people and wanted to be left alone. So we went to the beach with Mom for picnics a lot and that was a great place to get calm. It was good to get out of our house and not have people looking at us, or even around. And we all got pretty good at Frisbee that week.

One of our aunts stayed in town after everyone left. She lived in our house with us for six weeks. I think that was really great for Mom. She's very positive and helped us and Mom look at things in a happier way instead of being too sad. She helped Mom sell Dad's car and the boat and get our life going again. She took Mom to the grocery store, went to the bus stop, and other stuff. Mom didn't joke around or talk with her friends like she used to, but Aunt Cindy did. This gave Mom her space.

But sometimes we felt like we needed our own space. She went out by herself a lot and sometimes she did the errands for us. So then we had our own space. And she'd stay in the other room when Mom was putting us to bed. That's when we did a lot of crying and talking.

Allie: After the funeral, we had to light a big candle that lasted for seven days. It was kind of freaky to see it getting smaller and smaller, because it felt like Dad was getting farther and farther away from me. But since his soul was already in heaven, he was still in the same place. We cried a lot when the candle went out.

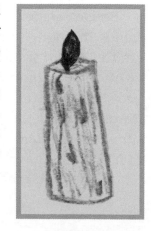

We weren't going to school, and when we weren't crying it was kind of fun. We spent a lot of time playing with new toys and games that people brought. It was pretty cool. It helped keep us busy, but it didn't get the sadness away when we were crying.

Mom told us that Dad's tests showed that his heart had an arrhythmia. That means your heart starts beating in the wrong rhythm and can't get back to the normal beat. It's hard to understand that. And Dad being only thirty-four years old and a doctor and in good shape—it doesn't make sense. But not everything can be cured, Mom said, and sometimes it's just like really, really bad luck.

LOOKING BACK

It's helpful to find out what your religion, if you have one, or your family says you should do when someone dies. There are lots of ceremonies and services and things that happen, and it's great to know what they are and why they're done. Once you understand the meaning of them, then they're not so bad. Like the *shiva* is so people can hang out together and talk about the dead person. You laugh and you cry, and then you feel better. And it kind of works. Probably most of the religious things are for that kind of reason, and once you know about them they might even help you.

Each family decides which religious rules they'll follow, like how long to do the *shiva*, that sort of thing. It was important to us that our grandfather let us do what we wanted to do about that without giving us a big lecture. And it was important to him that we did some of the things that he wanted, like having the prayers every day in the house. You have to respect each other's decisions, because everyone has their own opinions when it comes to religion.

Some religions require more stuff than others. And some people are not into any religion at all, or they have their own ideas about souls and spirits. Or maybe there are two religions in one family. You have to respect what others choose to do because you want them to respect what your choices are. You can't just be selfish and act like everything should revolve around you and your decisions, because it doesn't. And if you try to be understanding, maybe you'll all be able to compromise.

Communication is one of the most important things to help you get through this awful time. Everyone's head is in a different place and you won't know what anyone is thinking unless you discuss it. It helps you to understand their feelings and moods and lets them understand you. This is important for your immediate family and also for your extended family, and even your friends. And it always makes you feel better to talk out loud about what you're thinking.

We've always been very independent and like to do our own things. But all of our friends and relatives wanted to be able to help us. They felt bad that we were so sad and they wanted to make our life easier any way they could. So if there are things your friends and relatives can do to help you, it's good to let them know. Like some families ask a grandparent or an aunt to live with them until they get back on their feet. We had an aunt do some of the errands at the beginning for us and we all felt better. We saw our grandparents a lot and felt better when we saw that they were doing okay and surviving this bad time. And they felt the same way seeing us.

And it's important to let them know when you need your space and how to handle your sad moods. When our grandparents were baby-sitting us and we went into our room for space and a good cry, they learned to leave us alone. And that worked out just like we wanted it to and everyone was okay. But if we hadn't told them, they would never have known.

Allie, Pop (Mom's dad), Amy, and David, Thanksgiving, 1996

Two Weeks

Amy: After two weeks of staying home and trying to get ourselves together, we felt ready to go back to school. At first, I was really nervous and thought I wouldn't make it through the day. Some of the weird things were that instead of going on the bus like usual, Mom drove us to school. That way, we didn't have to put up with all the questions and looks from people. Most of my friends came over to me and said how they had grandparents who had died, or else they just ignored the whole subject. But there was no way of ignoring it, really. I could see the way they were looking at me differently, or whispering to each other, and I knew it was about me and The Situation.

My teacher was extra nice to me. Mom had said I could leave school early if I wanted or needed to, but once I was there it was okay and I made it through the day.

Now when people talk about their grandparents dying, though, I feel like they're looking for extra attention. I know it's kind of selfish, but I feel like I have a much worse situation and they shouldn't be that sad. At least their grandparent lived a long time. But I guess death is hard at any time, because it's just so difficult to deal with. The person is gone forever—that's such a tough thing. And there's really no point comparing who has it worst, who gets to be saddest. Grief isn't a contest.

In school, we were starting to work on science fair projects, which every student had to do independently. This was hard, because Dad was always great at science and had helped me do science projects in the past. My grandmother wanted to help me in place of my dad, but

I thought Mom could do it. If my grandmother helped me, I thought I might feel like an orphan. School projects are something that a parent helps you with, you know? We would have to manage ourselves, Dad or no Dad. That's when I realized that we *would* manage, even though it wouldn't be the same. Other people in my life could help with the things he used to do, but not exactly. I mean, my science project was fun and ended up being pretty good, but it wasn't the same type of fun doing it with Mom. She was more serious. If Dad had been around, it would have been really excellent.

Allie: During the first week, I thought I would never be able to stop crying. I mean, I had times when I was okay and even laughing, but then the tears would come without warning. I felt like that kind of thing would never stop.

But then one time I thought about not having Dad around and I didn't cry immediately. And I knew that I was going to get through it. The thing is, when nothing awful happens in your life, you think it might be interesting to have something happen just so you could get attention. But when it does happen, you realize that you don't want the attention and you're left with a big hole in your heart.

I've had a hard time with all the visitors coming over because I'm afraid I might start crying. When that happens, I go into my bedroom until I feel stronger. Mom tells people that I just need my own space. Sometimes, though, the person comes in because they want to help. And maybe they do help. But the best thing they could do would be to listen to what I'm asking, which is that I want to be left alone. It's hard not to get angry when they're butting in even after I tell them that I need my own space. If only they would just listen to what I'm saying.

I started to have a pain in my heart and I got pretty nervous about it. Mom took me to the doctor and he said it was nothing except sadness. I knew that, but I guess I felt better knowing that he checked me out and that my heart was in good shape. I mean, look at Dad. He thought his heart was okay and then he just died. Now I know that it won't happen to me because my heart is healthy.

LOOKING BACK

Once you go back to school, it's like life starts over again. It's important to not get too involved in feeling sorry for yourself, even though it's normal to do that sometimes. Your friends will get tired of you being sad if it's not really from your heart. Sometimes people keep whining about the same stuff just to keep getting attention. And of course there are still a lot of sad things to discuss about losing a parent as time goes by. But it's easy to tell when they're real feelings and when they're attention-getting feelings. And what good is that attention, really? It doesn't bring your parent back, and it doesn't make you happier or let you move on with your life and with the grieving thing.

It's important to not get angry at other kids because their lives are still normal and yours is so messed up. It's not their fault. And you know what? You don't know what's happened to them or to their families that may have been tough for them to deal with. Everyone has some bad stuff to deal with in life. Sometimes it happens when you're young and sometimes when you're older. Either way, you have to learn to deal with what comes along and get through it in order to go on.

Sometimes you might get mad at your parent for dying. And maybe it even was their fault, like if they were driving too fast or something like that. But being mad won't change the fact that they're dead. You have to deal with your feelings and know that everyone makes mistakes, some careless and some not. And some mistakes are worse than others and can cost a life. You can't help being angry if you are, because then you're not dealing with your feelings. You need to discuss how you feel with someone and let it all out. It won't change the fact that the person is dead, but you'll have handled it and can move on to other things.

Six Weeks

Allie: When I'm at school, the time goes by pretty fast and I don't usually even think about the Dad thing. Every once in a while, something is discussed that reminds me of it, but I make myself think about something else. I think it would be tough to start crying at school, because everyone would try to make me feel better but that would just make me cry more.

Sometimes we have to say a special prayer that people who are mourning say for the first year and then say on special holidays. It's hard to do it because it talks about the person being dead and how G—d is great. But if He is so great, then how come my dad is dead? I know there must be some reason, even if we don't get to know it. Maybe he was needed in heaven. Sometimes I imagine that he's working in the best doctor lab ever imagined and is finding the cure for cancer. G—d selected him because he was the best doctor on the whole earth. When he finds the cure, he'll tell another doctor in his dreams so he can wake up and cure the disease. But I'll know it was my dad who came up with the idea. I hope it's true.

It's hard to never know if it is or not. I feel so out of touch, if only I could just know Dad was okay and happy. But then I'd want to know more. It's hard to accept not knowing anything. I guess you just have to keep telling yourself that he's okay and pretty soon you start to believe it. Because you have to. And it's not like there's any proof that he's not okay, so I just think about his situation up there in a positive way.

Amy: Our aunt left a few days ago. She said she could stay longer and Mom was thinking about it, but we all said it was time to try living on our own, so she left. We've been doing pretty good, because time goes by and we have school stuff and all.

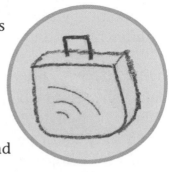

We see our grandparents a real lot because we're all they have left from Dad. We've always been close to them, but sometimes it's difficult to see them. They still cry a lot, which we do, too, but I don't really want to cry with them, only with David and Allie and Mom. It makes me sad to see them cry, and then I think about missing Dad and feel so lonely for him. And sometimes I feel very guilty that I'm not crying as much as they are. I know that I'm just as sad, because he was my dad, so I think that maybe I should make myself think about it more and cry more. But I'm not going to, because it's harder to be happy than it is to let myself be sad, and I feel like I'm doing a good job. And I know that Dad would want me to be happy whenever I could be.

Sometimes it's hard to deal with Dad's parents, because we're all a little jealous of them. After all, they had the most time with him—thirty-four years. Then Mom had sixteen and we only had since we were born. I wish so much that I had gotten to be with Dad for thirty-four years. So what are they crying about? I mean, I know it's still really sad for them, but it's sadder for us, and besides, we're his kids. But everyone has their own sadness and everyone is looking at it from their own point of view. I try to understand that they're sad in a different way, but it's still frustrating sometimes.

David: Amy lost a tooth, and in her note to the tooth fairy, she asked about how Dad is. It could be that they're both invisible and flying around in the sky. The tooth fairy said Dad was happy that we were doing so good and being brave about moving on. We were all happy to get the news. I'm lonely for Dad.

It might be a good idea to decide ahead of time how to handle a situation when you're with your friends and you start having a crying time. You may feel happy and like you're okay to go to school or to a friend's house, but then for some unknown reason you feel like you got punched in the face with a dose of complete sadness that you can't control, even though there wasn't even any mention of a father or anything that would make you sad. You just can't control yourself at all.

If you know you can reach your parent or a relative by phone or beeper, or reach someone else who can take you home, then it makes it easier. Or maybe you want your parent or relative to just let your friend's parent know that if you get sad you might want to go to a room and hang out by yourself until you feel like you can come out. Whatever works for you, it's good to figure it out ahead of time so you don't find yourself in an uncomfortable situation.

You might want to set up a meeting with your religious leader. He or she can answer your questions about death and the spirit and soul and all of that stuff. It helps to know about those things, because then it doesn't always feel so final. Even though Dad's body is dead, we believe that his soul is up in heaven and he can still see us. And that makes us feel better than when we first thought about it. At first, we felt like it was completely over and he was nothing anymore and that was a lot harder. Figure out what you believe, either from your religion or in your own heart. Then work it out so you can think about it in the most positive way that you can.

It's still important to communicate about the different feelings you have. Like if you're feeling guilty or jealous, then you should talk about that with your parent or whoever. We spoke with Mom and realized that there was nothing for us to ever feel guilty about. And after we spoke with our grandparents about feeling jealous of all the time they had with Dad, you know what we found out? They said they were actually jealous of us because Dad was so happy when we were around and always wanted to spend his free time with us. If we hadn't discussed it, we wouldn't know and then we'd all be secretly jealous and maybe even mad at each other.

Allie, Grammy (Dad's mom), and David
Washington, D.C., 4/01

David: Sometimes Mom lets us stay out of school for the day. It's usually when we stayed up really late at night talking or wake up with puffy eyes from too much crying. The nights are the hardest; we talk about Dad a lot and cry a lot then. It's still hard to believe that he's really dead.

Sometimes I think about what Dad's body is like now. I'm not sure if there are bugs that can get in the coffin. But he's under the ground, so they probably can, and his arms can't move to swat the bugs away. That's so awful and I feel so sorry for him that he's under-ground. I know that his body is just being recycled, like an empty soda can, now that his soul isn't there. But it's still Dad's face and body and it's hard to imagine.

Allie: We were taking a day off from school and went to the park with Mom's work partner and her kids. Amy fell off a jungle gym she was climbing on and broke her arm. Everyone was freaking out, so Mom had us all chill out for a few minutes and have a drink. Then she called the bone doctor and before we knew it we were in Dad's old office building. That was weird, because everyone there was sneaking by the room to check us out. Some of them came in to say

Amy with a broken arm

hello, but most just stared as they went by the room we were in.

It was weird that we had a medical situation and Dad wasn't around to help us with that. Mom isn't really that strong about health things, but she did pretty good. It was so sad not to have Dad there to be in control. What were we doing in his office building without him?

LOOKING BACK

Sometimes you need to take a break from the routine and clear your head. Of course, it depends on your parent's schedule what will work out best. We took a lot of weekend trips and it was great to get away. Then we didn't run into people we knew, which was good because they'd give us pity and ask how we were doing. Sometimes it's good to just get away from it all and be around people who don't know your situation. It wasn't like we were running away from it, because we were always talking about it and dealing with it. But it was nice to take a break from the sympathy looks every now and then.

Your parent or whoever you live with now may be able to take you out of school early or let you skip a day. This helps, too, even if you don't go anywhere. There's so much emotional energy that you're dealing with all the time. It's sometimes nice to take a total break and not have to work so hard at everything.

And around this time, you need to accept that there are new rules now that a member of your family is gone. Your parent may have to work a lot more now, since they're the only one earning money in the family. You might have to get used to them not being home as much, or you might have to go to an after-school program. You might have to do more jobs around the house to help out. Everyone has to pitch in and take over the dead parent's jobs. If you lost both your parents, maybe you're living with a relative or somebody else. It doesn't mean that you're going to be happy about it. You probably won't be.

Mom wasn't really happy about having to increase her work hours, but she had no choice so she just did it. And you may not have much choice, so you'll just have to do it, too. But make sure you talk about your feelings and maybe everyone can work out a compromise that's not too hard to live with.

And things will happen that you're used to having the dead parent handle, like the broken arm thing. Well, they can't handle it anymore and you'll all have to figure out new roles and new ways to deal with those situations. In the end, we didn't really freak out too much that we had to deal with a health emergency without Dad. And we did just fine. So don't make it more than it is and it won't be.

In the end, everything is manageable if you break it into small enough pieces and deal with one part at a time. And really, that's the best way to handle all the grief and the loss of your parent. At the beginning, it's just so big and overwhelming that you can't possibly deal with it all, so you deal with just a little bit at a time—that day, or just that hour, or maybe even just the next five minutes. You deal with that, and that's manageable. Then when that's over, you deal with the next small amount of time. Eventually, you can deal with more and more.

Three Months

Amy: A couple of things have happened lately. It was Mom's birthday. She said she didn't want a big celebration because it made her too sad to have a birthday without Dad around. We made her lots of cards. Aunt Cindy had taken us shopping for gifts before she left. Both of our grandparents and a few of Mom's friends asked us if they could take us shopping for the gift. It was like, enough already, back off! I guess it's nice that they want to be helpful, but we can all manage on our own.

Her birthday ended up being fun because we made all the plans and she was happy that we made an effort. It may not have been as perfect as if Dad had been around, but it was still okay. She was also pretty sad, though, which I can understand. She said she'd celebrated her birthdays with Dad since she was a teenager and it was hard that he wasn't around. I felt sorry for her that she was crying on her birthday.

For Mother's Day, Mom took us to the store we wanted to go to and then she waited in the front while we shopped. She'd given us her credit card and told the cashier that we'd be using it. She said we were buying a surprise present so the cashier should just ring it up and put it in the bag. Of course, that's not what happened. The lady held it up and said to Mom, "Is this what you're using the credit card for?" Mom was really angry at her and told us she didn't really see the thing, but we all knew that she had. Oh well, it's the thought that counts.

Allie: The doctor group that Dad was in moved into a new office building. Dad had taken us to it when it was being built and showed us which office would be his. He was so excited and proud about it. Well, they had a building ceremony and dedicated the atrium to Dad. We got new outfits and got to sit in the front row. Then after a few speeches, Mom got up and gave a speech. But here's the big thing: We got up with her and each said a few sentences. I wasn't sure that I wanted to do it, and Mom said if I decided not to, then I could just give her a nod and she'd keep talking.

When we were driving there, we heard one of Dad's favorite Pink Floyd songs and we knew he was with us. After that, I knew it would all be okay and I said my part during the speech. I got a little teary eyed but held myself together, even when they showed us a big plaque with Dad on it that was being hung on the wall. There was a sena- tor there, too. I was really proud of Dad.

The building dedication went fine, even though we were all pretty nervous about talking in front of so many people. But I know that Dad would have been really proud of us because a lot of his patients were there, and the other doctors he always bragged to about us. Mom started crying during her speech and she almost had to let her work partner take over. But then she got herself together and we were proud of her. Dad's parents were going out of town, but they said they thought it would be too hard for them to be there anyway.

David: We talked at the building dedication for Dad. I got to stand on a chair and talk into the microphone. I could hear myself breathe into it. It was hard to see Dad's picture smiling and so happy on the plaque but not really there. I was glad that we heard the Pink Floyd song because then I wasn't nervous anymore. We had to shake a lot of people's hands after the ceremony, and we all got the giggles. Some of the people were crying when they met us, so I guess giggling wasn't the best thing to do. But Mom didn't mind. And then we got to pig out on lots of brownies and cookies.

We talked about what would happen to us if Mom died. She said that one of her sisters would take care of us. We like them and they're a lot like Mom, so that would be okay, but so weird. I hope that she doesn't die until I'm older so that doesn't happen. I like the cousins and stuff, but I think it would be tough to live with them and be like sisters and brothers with them. Also, we didn't figure out how we'd get to the airport and buy a plane ticket to get there. So I hope that nothing happens.

LOOKING BACK

Celebrations are really tough, especially the first year. It's hard to be happy about an occasion because it feels so wrong to celebrate something when your parent isn't there. It's good to discuss ahead of time what kind of celebration to have. Mom wanted to ignore the holidays more than we did, so we compromised. Even though it was annoying that so many people wanted to take us shopping, it's still nice that they offered. They all just wanted to help and make it easier for us, which is really nice. So it's important to think about their feelings and say no thanks instead of getting too annoyed.

And the way we worked it out so we could shop ourselves and use Mom's credit card for Mother's Day was also a good solution. We were happy with that, because we could still kind of surprise Mom.

It was good that we talked about what would happen if Mom died. The three of us had discussed it without Mom, and then one day she just brought it up. That was great because it cleared up a lot of stuff for us and took the worry out of it. But we shouldn't have waited for her to bring it up and worried about it all that time. We learned that if we had something on our minds, we should just ask about it.

Four Months

David: I've been missing Dad a lot and thinking of lots of things that remind me of him. Like the other day we were driving in the car and we passed the marine store. I thought of all the fun times we had when we would go boating. Wednesday was the day Dad always left work early to pick us up from school. Mom would work later or do errands and we would have time with Dad. It was always so special. And it makes me sad to think we can never have that anymore.

Another thing is that *Star Wars* is showing. Luke Skywalker grew up without a dad and found out that Darth Vader was really his dad when he was grown-up. But I'm growing up without a dad, and that makes me sad. Especially because I'm not going to grow up and find out that there's anyone who is really my dad, because he's dead.

Dad and I had special boys-only times. Now there's no one to do just boy things. Sometimes Mom gives me time alone with her, but it's not the same. Why did this have to happen to my dad? There's more than a billion people in the world. And my dad cured people. He was such a nice man. It's not fair.

Amy: I have my up and down times, and the downs sometimes last an hour or a few days. If Dad was still around, things would go more smoothly. I

never had real down times when Dad was alive. Just little bummers here and there, like school things or friends. Not anything so big, like Dad being dead. It just seems like everything was sunnier with Dad in the world.

But I don't think about the Dad thing too much. Because when I do, I get really sad and I still can't believe that he's really gone forever. Even though it's been four months, I still can't really believe the whole thing. It's just too big to handle sometimes. And when it feels like that, it's better to sometimes think about other stuff. I let myself think of the Dad situation in my stronger times.

I try to look at the positives of the situation. For example, now Mom sleeps in our room every night with us. I mean, I don't blame her, since Dad died in her bed and everything. Lots of times she comes in kind of early or we stay up late, and then we all talk about how we're feeling. And talking in bed is good—it seems easier to say some things or talk and cry when it's dark in the room. Then no one's really looking at each other, just listening. That really, really helps. It's important to be able to talk with someone about what's in your head. It could be your parent or another relative, or a school counselor or a friend.

Allie: Mom spends more time on the phone than she used to. All of her friends are always calling to check up on her and make sure that she's okay. Sometimes she just turns off the answering machine and the phone ringer and then it doesn't bother any of us. I know she needs her friends, but it's annoying.

Mom says she would never be able to handle the Dad situation as well as she is without us, and that we're her inspiration. Since we're doing a good job dealing with it, and we were his kids, then she knows that she can do it, too. That makes me so proud when she says that. I think it helps a lot that we're all always talking about Dad and what we're thinking about. When you share what you're thinking about, then you realize that the people around you are feeling the same way. And once you've said it out loud you feel like it's easier to deal with. Just thinking it to yourself isn't usually enough to get it out of your mind.

LOOKING BACK

As time goes on and your life starts to get somewhat normal, you keep thinking, *Why did something like this have to happen to my family?* You might blame either of your parents, yourself, or someone else. In the end, there's usually no one to blame. And even if there is someone to blame, deal with it and move on. Everyone makes mistakes or does something wrong. This may have been a big, awful mistake, and sometimes there's no chance to apologize and ask for a second chance. So be angry if you feel that, even if it's at your dead parent, and get it out of your system. Then move past it and just accept the fact that they're gone without looking at the reason or being angry anymore. Things just happen and that's how life is. You have to accept some stuff without always having reasons for it. It's a really hard thing to do.

Accepting what's happened makes it easier to concentrate on the positives in your life. Learn to appreciate what you have and who you have in your life. There's so much good in your life, you have to constantly be thankful for it. And you realize that it's not so bad to lose one thing when you put it all into perspective, even if it is still a bummer. We're happy to have such a great

Mom and Zayde (Dad's dad), Washington, D.C., 4/01

family, to have such great grandparents and aunts and uncles, to have good friends, to all be healthy, to be able to understand things. There's a lot more good than there is bad.

And you find that being complimented on how you're doing is really important. You're spending so much time and energy on dealing with your emotions, trying to find happiness, working on not being too angry, all those things. So when someone tells you they're proud of you and you're doing a good job, it means a lot. And knowing that, it becomes important for you to compliment the other people in your family. If you have brothers and sisters, they're feeling the same way, and if you still have a parent, they're struggling as a single parent with double the work. Your grandparents are dealing with a dead child, and there are lots of other people dealing with their own loss. You can praise them for something that they're handling well and they'll feel really great, too.

Six Months

David: I'm getting used to life without Dad most of the time. I don't even think about him that much. Sometimes Mom asks me what I'm thinking about, and I don't usually say Dad. I'm busy at preschool in the day and then I play after school. I used to usually see Dad just before I went to sleep, so that's when I miss him the most. Then I think about hearing the garage door opening and his car pulling in, and I feel lonely that it won't be happening tonight.

The summer was fun because we did a lot of driving trips with Mom. We drove up to Canada, which is a whole different country. We live in Florida. There were lots of fun stops on the way. And we took a lot of week-end trips to different places in Florida. It was a fun time being together, but we all missed Dad a lot. We talk about him a lot, especially when we're all going to sleep at night. Then one of us usually starts crying and then we all do. But it feels good to talk about it, and we all feel better after that.

Amy: We all managed the rest of the school year, and it went okay. It was hard getting back the big test scores at the end of the year, because Dad should have been there for it. He would have been so proud of us. I feel like he knows about it, and that someday I'll meet him in heaven and we can talk about every-thing. But then I try to picture it and I can't. How will he know me if I die when I'm an old woman? And how can there be enough room for every single dead person? We talked to Mom's friend who's a rabbi and he gave us some answers. But mostly he said that you can't picture everything and that you just have to have faith that it will all be okay.

The summer trips were a lot of fun. It's easier to not think about Dad when we change our routine or go away. But then when the trip ends and we come home, it's really depressing. Sometimes I say to myself that it's been half a year already, when will I stop being so sad about his absence? I feel pretty confused about a lot of the death stuff, because I'm trying to imagine how it all works up in heaven. And I feel upset that this all hap-pened to my dad and to our family. He was such a kind man and spent so much of his time helping and healing other people. Why did this happen to our dad?

LOOKING BACK

The death of a parent is something that will always be with you. You can't expect to have a certain period of time to grieve and then put it all behind you. Each time something happens, throughout your life, you think about the person again. We're dealing with it so much better than we were at the beginning. But there will always be sad times, no matter what happens, through the rest of our lives. They may not be as sad or last as long as they do now, but they will be there. And it's okay as long as you expect it to happen.

Our talks about how we're feeling and about Dad in general are always really helpful. All three of us usually find out that we've been thinking about the same stuff, and that makes it easier, knowing that we're not sad alone. It's great to be able to discuss everything you're thinking. After all, your life changes so much when that parent isn't around.

We were able to talk to some doctors and ask questions about Dad and his heart. It was good to know that it probably won't happen to us, because we were all secretly concerned about that. And it helps to be able to understand the whole thing. I was glad when one of the doctors said that he probably never even knew what was happening and didn't feel anything. If we hadn't talked to them, we might not have found that out.

And it's important to learn a little bit about what your religion or family says about death and the soul. It helps you maybe get some comfort and understanding. Or whatever you think, whether it's religious or not. When you talk about this stuff out loud, then you really start to think about all of the questions you have. And once you learn how to answer them your own way, you can move a little bit away from total grief and begin to handle it.

Eight Months

Allie: We started third grade in a new elementary school on the other side of town. Mom thought it would be easier for us to be in a place where everyone hadn't lived through Dad's death. You know, kids were always pointing us out as the ones who'd lost their dad. And some of them were acting kind of uncomfortable around us and stuff. That was weird, because we were trying to just be our normal selves, but they weren't really letting us. Anytime the word *father* came up, everyone snuck peeks at me. It was awful. I always felt the tears in my eyes, but I usually managed to not blink so they wouldn't come out and no one would know.

I wasn't sure about changing schools because I didn't know any of the teachers and the routine—like how the lunch line works, that sort of thing. But by the end of the first day, everything was fine. I like the new school and the kids, and I've already made some friends. Some kids whispered to me that they know about Dad from their parents, but that was it. We didn't discuss it, and the rest of the class doesn't know. I actually do feel better now, because being treated differently was hard.

David: I started prekindergarten, which is the highest preschool grade. There were a lot of dads dropping off their kids, and I felt sad that my dad wasn't there. It's not fair.

I like my teachers and they think I'm smart. That makes me happy, because I feel like I have some of Dad's brain, which is good.

I don't cry too much anymore about the Dad thing. Mostly when I see my grandparents, because my grammy cries a lot. She's just an emotional person. Our grandfather is sad, too, but he tries really hard to be rowdy with us. They tell me it's hard for them, because Dad was their kid so they have a lot to be sad about. But seeing them cry makes it hard because then I feel like crying, too. We all miss Dad a real lot, but we're pretty proud that we're moving on in a positive way. Sometimes Mom reads us stories in the newspaper about a whole family that got badly hurt in an accident. Then it seems that just losing a dad isn't even such a big deal. But it is, because it's pretty lonely without him.

Amy: Mom didn't let us have any sleepovers this summer at our grandparents' houses. We always used to, and that was always really special and fun. She said she couldn't handle being home alone overnight and we would have to understand. It's hard to understand but I am trying.

Sometimes when I'm mad, I know I take it out on Mom. You know how you always blame your parents for stuff, even if it isn't their fault. I mean, I feel bad because lots of times I know it's not her fault. But I can't help it, and she tells me later that she knows I'm doing it because I'm just frustrated at the whole situation. I say I'm sorry and she already knows that, and then we go on. She's very understanding.

The first thing I had to do in my new class this year was bring in photographs of my family. Allie and David and I look through the photo albums every once in a while, but Mom never does. She says she's just not ready. I can understand that, since we always end up crying when we see the pictures of happy times with Dad. It's so hard to believe that he's really dead. Why did it have to happen to our great family? It's not fair.

But I know that other families have a lot of worse things and then someone dies on top of that. At least we were always happy. Things could have been worse and I try to remember that we're still lucky when I am feeling really sad. I mean, it could have been worse and Dad could have suffered. Or he could have died with Mom, or maybe before he had us. So I try to look at the things that I'm happy about and thankful for, and pretty soon the sadness goes away.

LOOKING BACK

If you feel like your friends are talking about your parent's death when you don't want to, then it's important to talk to them about it. They'll never know where your head is unless you tell them. Maybe they're trying to ask you about it because they think that's what you want. So if you just say, "I'd rather not talk about it unless I bring it up," then everyone understands what to do and it's easier to be together. Your friends want to have a normal relationship with you again but they're just not sure how to do it.

We've always been close with Dad's parents and still are. There have been rough times while we all deal with this terrible tragedy in our own ways. They have their own sadness and things to handle, and they deal with it in their own way, and we may do it differently. But in the end, we're all suffering from big broken hearts and it's nice to know that we're there for each other. It's important to be understanding about others' feelings, just like they are to yours. If you feel like their crying might be too much for you, maybe it's better to reschedule the plans you made. But if you discuss it openly and honestly, then your relationships don't have to suffer during this bad time. We try to help our grandmother look at the positives so she'll be happier. It makes her see things in a happier way, and then we're happy that we were able to help her.

You also have to be careful not to take things out on your family. People feel a lot of anger when someone dies. You might be angry that you have to work harder, that your life has changed, that you don't have as much money for toys and clothes, all sorts of different things. Or you just might be angry that it happened to your parent because you miss them so much and it's not fair. And it's not. But it happened and you need to find a way to calm yourself down. Don't take out your anger on another person, or on yourself. Find a way to just chill out. Maybe work out, meditate, read a book, anything that works for you. Because if you're always angry, then you'll end up alone, and that would be really bad.

The Cemetery

Amy: In the Jewish religion, we don't put the gravestone down until just before one year. It's called the unveiling. But we had to order the gravestone four months after Dad died. Mom said we could decide what to put on the stone as long as Dad's parents were okay with it.

We walked around the cemetery for a while and saw what most of the gravestones said. Not that we were going to copy their ideas, but just to see how some of the graphics and wording looked. We figured out our own words and then picked out what lettering and graphics to use. It was a hard decision because whatever we picked would be there forever.

At the unveiling, the stone is uncovered during a ceremony so relatives and friends can see what it looks like. It's supposed to be an end to the mourning period. Mom didn't want to have us go through a huge, sad ceremony, like at the funeral. Dad's brother and sister came down from up north, and his cousin came, too. All of our grandparents were there, but Mom told her sisters and friends not to come. My grandpa had prayer books for everyone and passed them out. We didn't want to make it a big deal, so we didn't even have a rabbi, we just did the prayers ourselves. Dad's parents were nice about letting us make most of the decisions. I know they had different ideas of how to do it. Then we uncovered the cloth that was over the grave and looked at the stone for a little while. Then we went home.

Actually, Mom took the three of us to see the gravestone before the day of the unveiling to let us handle it without anyone else around. Even though we knew exactly how it would look, it was still impossible to actually see his name there. What was my dad's name doing in a cemetery?

David: At first, when I went to visit Dad at the cemetery, I would draw him a picture and write "I love you" on it. Now I do sometimes and other times not. I feel like he's with me all the time and I don't need to bring him notes or pictures just to the cemetery. But I always have a conversation in my head with him when I'm there. You know, like what's happened since the last time I visited and how much I miss him.

We got to pick out how the words would be on the gravestone. But we didn't want Dad's middle name because he never used it and it's kind of weird. His parents really wanted it bad, so Mom said that we should compromise. That was hard because now it's not our way, and we're his kids. At first we were upset, because we only wanted it to be our way. But they compromised and that made it a lot easier on us. And our compromising made it easier on them. In the end, we were all okay with the final result.*

Sometimes we make different crafts to put around the gravestone, like one time we painted "World's Best Dad" on the backs of shells. Then we pushed them into the ground all around the stone. They lasted there for a while and then pretty soon some of the shells got lost and the letters didn't make sense anymore. We don't

---

*The gravestone has his full name and M.D., which his parents wanted, and some wording that they wanted ("Loving dad, husband, son, brother"). It also has some wording we wanted ("The love and memories you gave us will be with us always"), along with a Jewish star and a medical insignia combined with a heart.

bring flowers, but some other people do. But then it's sad when the flowers are dead.

Allie: The unveiling ceremony was very quick, which was easier for all of us. We were really sad on the car ride home from the ceremony. Mom said there was a surprise hidden in the car and we found concert tickets under the floor mat for that night. That was a great way to get out of the unhappy mood.

LOOKING BACK

We were really happy to have been the ones to make most of the decisions about the gravestone. Even though we didn't want it exactly how it ended up, we all got most of what we wanted. It's important to compromise, because everyone has their own ideas of how things should be and there can only be one gravestone, one ceremony, one whatever. If everyone stays calm and works together, then you can all be pretty okay with the end result. If you throw a fit and only say it has to be your way, chances are you'll still have to compromise anyway but you'll feel bad about it.

It was important for Dad's parents to make some of the decisions about the stone and the unveiling ceremony.

They were his parents, so they need to make some of the decisions, too. Sometimes you get involved in thinking your grief is more important than anyone else's and your decision should count more. Everyone grieves in their own way, and no one kind of grief is worse than another. A broken heart is a broken heart. There's no point in making someone who's sad even more miserable by having a fight.

It helped to know ahead of time what the unveiling would be like. We were happy to have gone to see the gravestone before the ceremony, when we were by ourselves. It was a pretty hard thing to see, and it was good to be alone the first time we saw it. Even if it bent the rules a little bit, in the end it was really helpful. So for us, it was okay.

Some of Mom and Dad's friends felt bad that they weren't invited to the unveiling. But we all felt that it was a private thing and we didn't want to make it a bigger deal than it had to be. And it really made it much easier for us that it was quick and simple.

One Year

Amy: We've almost finished half of a new school year without Dad being around. When kids ask me questions about my dad, I say something like, "I don't really want to talk about it now," or, "Well, he's not around." I used to say that he was away at meetings and stuff, but Mom said that was a lie and not a good thing to do, especially if someone knew the truth. I don't like to tell anyone the truth because I don't really like to talk about it with them. I'm afraid I might end up crying or they might start treating me differently. I really don't like the way people react, because then I don't know what to say. Like when they say, "Oh, Amy, I'm so sorry," what am I supposed to say?

I wonder sometimes what Dad would be thinking or saying. We visit the cemetery once or twice a month. Sometimes I draw a picture or write Dad a letter, but not every time. When we go, I usually don't cry anymore. Sometimes I try to remember what his voice sounded like, but I usually can't. I can remember what Dad would say, but not exactly what it would sound like. So that freaks me out, but I know it will come back into my mind eventually. I just wish it would already. We try to watch home movies but it's so sad. I feel like it was just a minute ago that we were doing the things we see with him. And I also feel like it's been so long since we've seen him and I almost feel strange seeing him on the movies, like I don't really know him or remember the way he was.

David: I talk to Dad sometimes, mostly at night and in the morning. Or sometimes around dinnertime. Like, "Good morning," "Good night," if there's anything new up there, stuff like that. I don't miss him all the time because then I would never have any happy time.

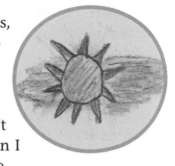

I only had four years with him and I feel like that's not fair because it's not enough time. Then Dad died and broke our family into pieces. But I feel like our family is whole now and that we're doing okay on our own. It would still be much better if Dad was around. It was always special to have five people in our family because most people only have four. So now I don't feel special about that anymore. But I know that we're going to make it and be fine, just the four of us.

We went away the week of February 9, even though we missed school. That was Dad's birthday, and then we didn't come back until after Valentine's Day. It was a hard week and we all cried a lot. It was sad not to celebrate Dad's birthday and to think that we will never celebrate it again. On the anniversary of the day Dad died, we went to a park and just hiked and hung out. It made the day easier, but it still was awful. We all were thinking about what the year before was like, and that was freaking us out.

Allie: When I see someone with their dad, I get jealous at first. But then I always think that my dad was the best and that I wouldn't want to be stuck with their dad anyway.

When I think of Dad, I try to feel happy, even though at the beginning it seemed impossible. I still cry at times, and I'm sure I always will have sad and crying times. I feel like my family will never be whole again. I talk to Dad whenever I want—it doesn't have to be at the cemetery. I have a picture of him on my bulletin board that I look at a lot. Then I think about stuff and I feel like he can hear me. Sometimes I can hear him encouraging me to do something in my brain, even though I can't quite remember his voice.

Even though my grandparents are sad a lot, which can be a bummer, I try to remember that they miss Dad, too. So then I try to be extra nice. It's just hard when my grandma is always crying. If I'm having a happy time and I see that, then I feel immediately sad. And I get annoyed with her for that, even if she can't help it. But then I get sad for her that she can't find happiness in other things. My grandpa stopped smoking, which he'd been trying to do for years. Dad always tried different things to get him to stop, and now I think what made him stop is that he wants Dad to be proud of him. I know that Dad is really proud, but it's sad that he can't tell my grandpa.

Mom's mom doesn't really talk to us about anything connected with the Dad issue. She was only his mother-in-law and it just isn't the same for her. We're very close to her and have a fun time when we're with her. It's good to be happy and forget about the Dad thing sometimes.

We went away during the anniversary of Dad's death. Right after Christmas, the stores had started getting all their Valentine's Day cards and gifts on the shelves. So that was a hard thing because there it was, right in our faces, that the hard day was coming. We decided to go somewhere outside so we wouldn't have to see a lot of valentine stuff. I kept thinking about what Dad was doing last year and how he didn't know that his time was almost up. In the end, the day wasn't as bad as I thought it would be.

Two days later, on the anniversary of his funeral, I couldn't keep my eyes off the clock. This was when he had his funeral, this is when we were riding to the cemetery—that kind of thing. I guess each year it will be a hard day, but it will get easier each time.

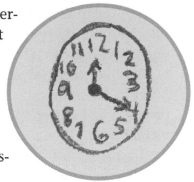

LOOKING BACK

We've had a pretty hard time watching the home movies. But when we do, then there's Dad, right on the TV. We hear his voice and see him moving around, and it's such a good way to remember. You have to pick a time when you're feeling pretty strong, though, because it's such a tough thing to see. It's great, but it's also extremely sad, because he's right there and he's looking so alive but you know that he's really dead.

The reason you can't remember his face or his voice or whatever is because you're not ready to deal with it. It's still too painful and you need to give yourself time. You have to know that it will eventually come back when your mind is ready to handle it. It's in there, but it's taking a break until the right time.

When you lose a parent, you have a long period of grieving time before you can move on. But eventually, the remainder of your family has to regroup and start moving forward again. Sometimes a grandparent moves in, or a live-in baby-sitter. Things are going to change, and you need to be prepared for it. So you have to keep discussing how you feel about it and what your needs are so that everyone is feeling okay. If someone has moved into your home, then having your own space may become more important, so you have to tell everyone and work out a solution.

Anniversaries of the death, birthdays of the dead parent—those are always going to be hard days. They'll probably get easier each year, but they'll never be completely happy times. Work with your family to figure out the best way to handle them. We were all happy to get out of town so we could be on our own, but some people will want to hang out with the extended family or with close friends. Others may spend the day at the cemetery or the parent's favorite places to remember them. Whatever works will be what's best for you.

And you shouldn't lie about not having a dad, like saying he's away or something like that. Maybe a friend's mom is driving the two of you home from school and she'll ask you about your family and it will make you uncomfortable if you aren't prepared. Discuss it with your parent or someone and decide on the best way to explain. Maybe even rehearse the conversation in your head. Then when it comes up, you know what to say, so it won't be too upsetting and you can end the discussion if you want to.

Fifteen Months

David: We've been camping a lot these days. We went a few times with Dad and all had a really great time. One time, we went to a campsite on the beach for Mother's Day. But Dad forgot the tent poles, so we stayed in a hotel, and we all always laughed about it.

Dad always injoyed camping it was one of his favorite things to do. He also loved his camping hat.

Amy's drawing of camping with Dad

Mom is pretty good about the camping thing, even though she hates bugs and always ends up getting hurt when she's putting up the tent. Sometimes she curses, and I don't like that, but she says she's trying to stop. We all like camping because we

Allie, Amy, and David canoeing in the Florida Keys, 12/96

don't have to take showers and we have lots of time together without TV or phone or anything.

Mom has been working a lot more than she used to when Dad was around. She says she needs to work more to pay the bills. But I get mad and frustrated sometimes about that. When Amy and Allie were five, she was always around and didn't work so much. It's kind of not fair.

Amy: Allie, David, and I have been working on a campaign to get cigarette butts off of the beaches. We adopted a beach and noticed that most of the litter was butts, and they're harmful to sea and land creatures. Well, last month we got honored by the mayor at a City Council meeting for the work that we've done.

It was incredibly exciting, and we each got to talk into the microphone and everything. And there were newspapers and tele-vision reporters who did

Allie, Amy, and David working on their "No Butts About It" campaign, 4/97

stories on us. A lot of the kids in school said they were jealous of me. I thought, *I'll never say that to anyone.* It's so stupid that someone would be jealous of me for being a little famous when I don't have a father. I would trade it in a second if I could, for even just five more Dad minutes. Or even for one hug.

It was sad that Dad wasn't there for that, but we knew he was around anyway. There was a favorite song of his on the radio the minute we got into our car to go to the ceremony, so we knew that he'd be there. But I wish I could have seen his happy face, because I know he'd be really proud of me. One time when he was around, there was a really small article in the news about a field trip that we'd organized to the beach and it said our names. He helped us cut it out and frame it and was showing everyone at work. If only he'd been here for our pictures on the front page and on TV, he would have been SO into it.

Allie: While we were at the City Council meeting, we had to wait our turn for the presentation. Right before us, they gave an award to the Emergency Medical Services people. Of course, they talked about when people call 911 and how emergencies are sometimes happy when you have good EMS people. All I could think was how it didn't matter what kind of EMS people came to our house because it turned out so sad.

We were all so proud of ourselves at the meeting, though, and the room was full of people. I only wanted one other person there, but of course he couldn't make it. Mom is pretty sentimental and cries a lot at those kind of things, and at school awards and stuff. So we try to leave her alone and after a few minutes she's okay. She tries hard to keep herself together and wears dark sunglasses so no one can see her tears, but they can tell something isn't right because she's wearing sunglasses inside.

After the meeting, a reporter interviewed us and took pictures. We felt so important. When we got home Mom had arranged a surprise party. It was so great!

That night, we were all in bed talking. We were getting sad about the Dad thing and how we wished he was there. Just then, the lights went out for about a minute. There wasn't any wind or rain or anything. And then they came back on. We all felt happy because we thought that was a message from Dad to let us know he was around.

We're all looking forward to the summer and thinking about what trips we'll take. Mom works from home and has a really great work partner, who's one of her best friends, so she can go away whenever she wants. We'll probably take a few driving trips and do a lot of hanging out and craft projects and things. Summers are always easier times because there's no schedule.

LOOKING BACK

When a family goes from having two parents to having one parent, there's a lot more stress on the parent who's still around. They have to work harder and earn more money, they have to make all the plans and do all the driving, and they have to be responsible all the time for the kids. So we try to remember that Mom is having a tough time, too, and help her out.

If you still have one parent and if you can just do one little thing for your parent each day, it would be a huge help. Or if you can do one thing for whoever you live with now, it would make them feel really great that you're being considerate and thinking of them. And you'll feel good, too.

We worked out a special signal for Dad during important times. We tap our shoulder and feel that he's paying closer attention. You might want to work out your own special signal, because it makes you feel like your parent is closer to you.

We all communicate in our heads with Dad. Maybe he can hear it and maybe he can't, but we think that he can and you know what? No one can say for sure what the truth is, so why not think that he can hear our thoughts? It brings him closer to us and makes us feel less lonely for him.

When we were getting the award or when we're trying for something, we're always motivated by thinking of how proud Dad would be of us. He may not be able to actually say, "Oh, I'm so proud," but he can tell us in other ways. A song on the radio that was his favorite, a rainbow—we look at those things as signs from him. And it feels great.

Allie, Amy, Mom, and David at the White House in Washington, D.C., for a ceremony where they received a President's award for their campaign, 4/01

Allie: This summer, David and Amy and I flew up to see Mom's dad, Pop, in Connecticut for a few days and Mom didn't come. I was excited to go on the trip until the very

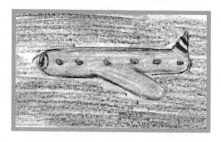

last minute at the airport, when we were boarding. I got nervous that I was going to miss Mom, and that something might go wrong on the plane.

When Mom left the plane because it was time to take off, I was crying. I had a big book, so I just held it and pretended I was reading. Amy was crying, too, but David was really excited to be one of the Dennison Adventurers. But he ended up crying in the middle of the plane ride.

We've been doing a lot of fun things this summer, and making our own camp activities. Mom usually works in the morning and we do our own craft projects. Then we swim or go somewhere and have a great time. It's easier to not miss Dad in the summer because we're busy until late at night, and then we're so tired that there's not much thinking time or feeling sad time.

David: We were all really excited to be the Dennison Adventurers and travel alone all the way to Connecticut. We got seats in the thirteenth row because we're only kids. That was pretty cool because we could see the pilot and the front of the plane.

It felt cool being by ourselves at the beginning of the trip, but toward the middle I got lonely for Mom. Mom said we could call her on the phone anytime, even on the plane if we wanted. But we didn't use the plane phone because it's so expensive.

When we got there, the first thing we did was call Mom. This was the longest I've been away from her since Dad died. I think that's most of the reason that I was nervous. We did a lot of fun things and finally, after two days, we drove over to Mom's sister's house. Mom had flown up and we all hung out with our cousins. The rest of the trip was great, but I thought of Dad a lot and what he would be saying and things like that.

LOOKING BACK

Staying busy is a really good way to help the time go by. The saying is, "All things heal with time," and it's true. We're still sad, but things are a lot better than they were when it first happened. We try to always have a few projects going, something to do on the computer, a sport to play, always something to do. That way we don't have too much sitting around and feeling sad time. There's enough of that anyway.

We never used to see Dad's family as much as we do these days, but that's part of the whole change in relationships. They need us a lot more these days as a connection to Dad. And we may need them more, too. Either way, it's nice to keep up a good relationship, because that's probably what your parent would have wanted you to do. And if you can help someone be happier by just being with them, then you should try to do it.

A Year and a Half

Amy: Yesterday we went to the cemetery with rocks that we'd painted. Each rock had a special pattern on it, and different colors. We used lots of purple because that was Dad's favorite color. We dug them into the ground so they bordered the gravestone.

When we were there, there was a grave set up for a funeral that was going to be held in a little while. The stand for the coffin was already set up, and we looked into the hole and saw the cement grave liner. The chairs were set up, too. It made me think back to Dad's funeral and when Mom fainted. It was so weird. I'm glad that it's behind us—that was such a tough time. I can't even believe how awful it was, like living in a nightmare. And then I think, *We're still living the nightmare because Dad's still dead.* But when it first happened, I never would have imagined I'd be living pretty normally again. And I am. So I'm proud about that. It's the hardest thing I've ever done, to go on living a normal life without Dad. But it really just happens if you let it.

I'm in the fourth grade now, and school is going pretty well. I'm in the top honors classes and I feel really proud about that. I wish Dad was around so our life would be normal like it used to be. We have a good routine and do everything we want to do, and a lot of times I'm okay with the whole Dad issue. But it's just not the same, and it never will be. And that makes me so sad, because no matter what happens, he can never come back. I feel so sorry for him that he lived such a short time and that he's not able to do fun things with us. I know that he'd want us to do them anyway, without him, and have a great time, but every once in a while I'll look around and see a kid holding hands with her father and I miss him so much.

Allie: School this year is harder but I know that I'll manage. I got pushed a year ahead in math, which I'm pretty proud of. Dad was great in math, so it makes me happy to think part of him is in me. I wish there was some way to get him back.

The teachers this year are nice, I guess. Mom and I discussed whether to tell the teacher about Dad and we decided that Mom should just write a note to let her know. She asked the teacher not to really discuss it with me but said she just wanted to let her know in case I had any Dad days or anything like that. The teacher was pretty cool, because she didn't talk to me about it, which is what I wanted.

Mom's work is doing really well and I'm proud of her for that. She spends a lot of time at the computer and on the phone with clients. Sometimes I need her help for homework and I have to wait, which is kind of a pain. I'm getting used to it, though, and she doesn't really have any choice. It's better that she's working at home than at an office. This way, she can change her schedule sometimes to come into school and things like that.

David: I'm starting to remember Dad a little bit more every day, but I still don't remember how he was. I talk to Mom in private a lot, like telling her that I miss Dad and things like that. I think about him a lot and Mom says it's important to talk about what we're feeling and thinking. Whenever I think of Dad, I run to Mom and say, "Mom, I'm thinking of Dad," or "DD," which is short for *dead Dad*. She says okay and then I go back to playing. Sometimes we both smile, like it's a game, but I really do feel better letting her know. She said I don't have to tell her every time, only when I want to talk about him. But I like to see how fast I can tell her and run back to my game without missing my turn.

I wish Dad could come back and see me because I'm playing soccer now. All the other kids have their dad there but mine isn't. Mom always comes and sometimes my grandpa comes. But that reminds me that the only boy there for me is my grandpa, and my dad is really dead. I know that my grandpa is really proud of me and is there to make me feel good, so I try to make a big deal out of it.

I started kindergarten this year and I'm happy about it. It's much more grown-up than preschool and I like my teacher. For the conference with her and Mom, I asked Mom to talk to her about the Dad thing—just in case I might start crying or something, I wanted to be able to go home. Mom told her and she was really nice about it and said I could go home whenever I needed to. But so far, I haven't needed to.

My sisters always talk about when they had their first days of school and Dad was always there with them at the bus stop. He would take them on rounds in the hospital before school so they wouldn't think about being nervous. I feel sad that Dad never took me on rounds, and that he's not here for my first day of school.

At my birthday, I always wish on my candle that Dad would come back. I know Amy and Allie wish this, too. We all pretty much know that it won't work, but that's what we want more than anything, so we keep wishing for it. I miss Dad a real lot these days. I can't believe it's so long already and I still miss him so much.

Dad, Amy, Allie, and David, 10/95

LOOKING BACK

You have to accept the fact that your life will never go back to the way it was before your parent died. Some things will change, and of course you've changed a lot. Besides being older, you've gone through a very hard thing and aren't the same person you once were. There's a lot left of life for you, and it can be a great life if you let it be. Always give yourself a break if you're feeling sad, because that's a natural thing, no matter how long it's been since your parent died. And appreciate how far you've come and be proud of yourself for it. It's not an easy thing to live through the death of a parent. Most people don't have to deal with it until they're parents themselves, and they still have a bad time handling it. You're only a kid and you're doing it, so be proud of yourself. And know that if you've come this far, you can handle anything.

Each time you change a grade or go to a new school, you'll have new kids and new situations to deal with. Try to prepare yourself ahead of time and think of what you want to say in each situation. Having Mom write a note to the teacher was a good way for us to handle it without having to actually say anything to the teacher ourselves. Of course, you can't be prepared for everything that will happen, but it makes it easier if you have a general idea.

Eventually you accept the fact that your parent is really gone and is never going to come back to you. And you realize that you've known that pretty much from the beginning and that you're handling it. And that's a great thing. It helps to be able to communicate with your dead parent in your thoughts, or in a journal, or somewhere. It helps you to deal with your feelings, too. And then you can keep moving forward.

Twenty-Two Months

David: We went to Connecticut like always for Thanksgiving, but this time we visited Dad's sister in Vermont first. We took a long train ride (six hours) and it was a lot of fun. It would be fun to live where there's snow, so we might move in the summer. I think that would be good but also bad. I would miss going to Dad's grave and knowing that his body is near me.

Valentine's Day cards are already in the stores. It makes me sad to see them because I think of how sad Valentine's Day will always be for me. Mom said she doesn't want to celebrate Valentine's Day but that if I want to make her a card it's okay with her. We were trying to decide if we should go away then, but Amy and Allie have a big test so we're going to stay around. I don't want to miss the Valentine's Day party at school—there's always a lot of candy.

Allie: Sometimes it's hard to be extra considerate to all of our relatives. They're sad and missing Dad a lot, too, and since we're a part of him and we're his kids, it's important to see them if they're around. Sometimes when a parent dies, kids lose touch with the parent's family, but if the kids keep seeing them, then the family won't have to worry about that happening.

But it's hard to squeeze everyone in, and I don't understand why Mom can't just say no sometimes. For example, we can't go away over Christmas vacation because Dad's brother is coming to town. But when Dad was around, we used to go away for part of that visit. It's annoying of Mom but she won't change on that.

The second-year anniversary is right around the corner and there's Valentine's Day stuff all over the place already. Some kids in my grade already like boys and talk about wanting a special card for that day. I wonder what I'll do about those kind of things.

We are going to be in town this year for Dad's birthday and death anniversary. We probably won't go to the cemetery those exact days because it would be too hard. Amy and David and I all think that we can handle going to school the day before Valentine's Day for our school parties, so we're going to try it. We talked about it one night and all decided that we really want to go, mostly because of all the candy, but we're not sure if we feel guilty. Last year, we would never have thought of going. It's our worst day of the year. But I guess that's a moving-on thing, so it's a good thing.

Amy: We talked about Mom starting to date sometime. I want her to have someone to hang out with, because it's sad that she's alone at night when we go to sleep, and I know that she's lonely, but it's hard to imagine someone else besides Dad around. I don't know if I could get used to that, and I might feel upset that someone's taking his place.

Mom says that she's still not ready to date, although a few of her widow friends have been dating for a while. Someday when we're all ready, she will. But she said she won't hang out with anyone we don't also like, so that's good. I guess it's one of those things that we can't really imagine until it happens, and then hopefully it won't be so bad. Maybe Dad will send someone who'll be really great and understanding about our feelings.

Someday your parent may want to get married again, or at least date. That's normal, and it's probably better than if they don't and just stay sad and lonely. But of course it's a hard thing for a kid to deal with, especially in our situation.

If you all talk about it, then it may not happen until you feel ready. And even if your parent is dating, that doesn't mean that you have to be part of it. It would be good if you can choose to meet the person when *you're* ready, even if your parent was ready earlier than you.

Just like you thought you'd never smile again after one parent died, your parent dating will be something that you'll eventually be okay with. It just takes time, and everyone works at their own speed. Don't rush yourself. When you're ready to meet the person or deal with the issue, that's when it's the right time. It's important to let your parent know how you feel and it's important to all respect each other's feelings. And if your parent is ready to date, then try not to make a big fuss. Let your parent move on with life, because that's a good way to be.

The most important thing, as always, is to communicate with each other and discuss things that are happening and things that are on your mind. And discuss your thoughts with your dad's family, if you're close enough to them. Once they feel secure that you'll always be there for them, then everyone can relax a little. They just want to love you and protect you, like all your relatives do. You may want your independence, but if everyone knows where they stand and how you feel it will be much easier.

Messages from Dad

Amy: If we ever see a rainbow in the sky when we're driving, I believe it's a sign from Dad telling us that we're doing great. There are other signs, too—like certain songs on the radio, a black Z-28 Camaro like Dad drove, and other things like that.

One time, on David's birthday, we had concert tickets to see David's favorite band, Aerosmith. We had fairly good seats. When we were waiting in line for a pretzel, a man with a Concert Staff nametag came up to

us and said he had tickets for the front row and would we like them? I thought this had to be a sign from Dad. Then during the concert, the bass guitarist gave my brother a high five and kept winking at the three of us all through the show. And Steven Tyler, the lead singer, touched Allie's and my hands!

Allie, Amy, and David dressed as rock stars for Halloween, 1996

David: We also had another message from Dad at the Aerosmith concert. One of Dad's favorite songs was "All Along the Watchtower" by Jimi Hendrix, and before the concert started they played that song.

I like getting the messages from Dad because then I'm sure he's around and watching us. Like we shoot off model rockets sometimes. We make them ourselves without a kit, and each time we make different style wings and bodies and stuff. One time, we were all feeling kind of sad and decided to shoot off rockets to cheer up. Mom took us to the college parking lot, and when we shot up the first one, there was a teeny little rainbow that appeared right where it went up. It only lasted for a minute and then disappeared. So we thought that was cool. And then we shot up the second rocket and we saw a double rainbow. So we all felt happy because we knew that would be a Dad sign. But then later we felt kind of sad because we all wished we could have more from Dad than a rainbow. Like a hug or kiss.

Allie: We don't really talk with too many people about the different signs that Dad gives us, because they don't usually understand. My grandfather looks at things only from the religious point of view. But who knows if a dead person can give people on Earth messages? I don't really know if they can, but I don't really know that they can't. In my head, sometimes I'm not sure if I believe it or if maybe it's just a coincidence. But I feel so happy and I guess I think it could be from Dad. A double rainbow would definitely be something that Dad would do if he wanted us to think about him.

Grandparents

Allie: Our grandparents live about ten minutes from us. There are goods and bads to that. It used to be a lot more fun to hang out with them. Now, seeing them is not as much fun because they cry a lot and are sad. Mostly Dad's mom. I know they try to hide it but it's easy to see. They need our support because they're not handling it as well as we are, and they're suffering their own loss. Still, sometimes I get mad that they're so sad. He wasn't living in their house and wasn't *their* dad, so their life didn't change as much as ours. I know it's not a contest about who's sadder, but it's just frustrating sometimes. We try to be understanding and remind ourselves that their healing time may be longer than ours.

Grammy, Dad's mom, cries the most, and she gets sad about every little thing. She has to try to get herself together because that's part of handling the loss. A lot of things we do could make us sad, but we look at the positives of it and try to find the happiness. Some days we have to try harder than other days to find it, but it can always be found if we try hard enough. She has to try harder, and she pretty much has been lately. She laughs more and doesn't cry EVERY time we see her, which is an improvement. Sometimes we joke around about her crying, even though we know it's mean. But it's a way of dealing with it, I guess. Mom gets mad when we do that but we can't always help it. And at least we're not mad at her.

The thing about our grandparents is that we've always been really close to them. So when this happened, they wanted to help us deal with it. We know their offers were out of love for us, but we wanted to still be a whole, independent family and let the hole seal itself up. We didn't need or want any other fifth person to fill in Dad's place. Some families want that additional person, and that's good if that's what you need. But to us, our grandparents' offers of help at the beginning felt almost like a threat to us.

In the end, the family that you have left needs to rearrange itself, with or without others. But you need to get your own new balance. Once we did that, then we could let them help without it interfering with our family space. It was good that we talked about how we were feeling with them so they understood us. Sometimes they didn't listen at first, but eventually they would. And once everyone knows where they stand, then they can all adjust their behavior so it works best and everyone can be happy.

Amy: My grandfather is handling it well. He's dealing with it better than Grammy and I haven't seen him cry too much lately. But sometimes his eyes get watery and then he goes outside. We never say anything about it and he probably thinks we don't see it.

Baba, our other grand-mother, was always really close to Dad, but she's Mom's mom so it's different for her. She asks us questions at times, but she never really talks about him, which is good. I would be afraid that if she did she might be saying different stuff than Mom,

Amy, Allie, and David with
Baba (Mom's mom), 2/97

and I wouldn't like that very much. It's good that all the grandparents know when to back off on different subjects.

Sometimes it's hard to ask Dad's parents questions about him because they get depressed. Not always, but there's a heaviness that changes the mood for a while. It's sad for them because they remember him when he was little. There's nothing we can do for them except to be nice, which we are. We usually go and play cards or just change the subject and ignore it. Eventually it passes and we can have fun again.

They're getting better about holding in their tears around us, so that's good. I don't expect them to hold their tears in all the time. Everyone has sad times and you need to let it out. But if someone cries *every* time, it gets tiring.

Dad's sister and brother come to visit from other states every once in a while. We're closer to Dad's sister. Sometimes she starts crying a lot when she's telling us stuff about Dad. It's hard to imagine having a brother or sister die. Allie and David and I are such a team, and if one of us died it would be so awful.

David: Mom gets along with all of our grandparents and tries hard to be understanding. She's always on the phone with Grammy and trying to let her talk about why she's sad. I think it must be hard for Mom. Sometimes when she gets off the phone she seems pretty bummed out. Then I feel mad that Grammy got her sad because it's a lot of work to stay happy. But we all need to be there for each other and Mom is just doing her part for Grammy. She says she feels happy to help Grammy and everyone needs to pour their heart out to someone. When I help my sisters or my mom be happy or let them talk, then I feel happy, too.

The Future

David: I'm sad that I'm going to grow up without a dad. There will be some new inventions and things and that makes me feel sad for Dad that he won't be around to see them and try them out. Dad and I always used to do things, just the boys. Sometimes Amy and Allie would even be jealous of that, but that's how it was. Now I can't do that with anyone.

And it's hard to be the only boy in the house. For sports, public bathrooms, stuff like that, a boy sometimes needs his dad. But Mom does that stuff with me and she's pretty good at most of it. She coached my soccer team and that was fun. It would have been better if it was Dad, but maybe he wouldn't have done it because of his work schedule. He was on call some weekends so he wouldn't be able to be there for every game.

Amy: Now and then I think about all those major things coming up, like *bat mitzvahs*,* my college graduation, my wedding, and all that junk. I can't imagine what they'll be like without him. When I get an award or am in a performance at school, it's hard without him. I know that he's around somewhere and that he's with me and watching me. We all tap our shoulder as a secret signal to him. Allie did it each time before her turn during the school spelling bee and she won. But, you know, it's not the same as him being there to give me a big hug and a smile.

We might move to Connecticut and I think that's exciting. I like the weather up there and my cousins and

---

*A *bat mitzvah* is the Jewish ceremony that marks a thirteen-year-old girl's transition to adulthood.

aunts and uncles are there. But then I'm not excited about it because Dad's grave is down here and all my friends are down here. I hope that someday maybe we can move him up to Connecticut if we move there. Mom said that wouldn't be fair to his parents. But we're his kids. He used to live with us, not them. It's one of those things we need to be understanding about. Anyway, I try to remember that he's with me everywhere I am and I can talk to him in my head. I don't have to be at the cemetery to do that. So it shouldn't matter too much. But it still sometimes does.

It's hard to imagine that maybe sometime in the future we might be having someone that Mom marries live with us. What if he has kids? Some of our friends have parents who were divorced and then remarried. That would be pretty much of a bummer to have new kids living with us. But I guess you can't begin to imagine that kind of thing until it happens. And if we don't all get along and don't feel it's the right thing to do, then I know Mom wouldn't do it. Anyway, we'll probably be the ones pushing her to date and move on because she doesn't seem too into it at all. I don't want her to be lonely, but I don't want us to change our lifestyles again. So we'll just have to be mellow and handle it as it comes along. As long as we all deal with things openly and honestly, then it will all work out okay.

Allie: I feel confident that the Dolphins will win the Super Bowl sometime soon. It was Dad who taught us how to watch a football game. You know, the rules and stuff, so it's hard that he's not here to watch it with us. We used to all cuddle in a blanket and watch the games on Sunday afternoons. We called the blanket "the football tent." I asked Mom to do it with us but she said no. It was too much of a Dad thing and it wouldn't be the same without him. We can do similar things, but they should be a little different so we don't ruin the memories of special things that were just with Dad. So we might sew a new football blanket for games in the future.

It would be hard to move to Connecticut, because there are a lot of memories from Dad in our house that we can't take with us. For instance, we surprised him with a new rug in the den on his birthday. Another year, we painted a mural on a wall for his birthday and we can't move that. We started tracing the old one, but then we decided it won't ever be the same. Mom said we could paint a different mural in our new house. That would be fun. Anyway, they're just things. The most important stuff is our memories and feelings, and those go with us wherever we are.

There are a lot of big things in my life that I'll have to handle without Dad being around, and that makes me sad. I sometimes think I won't even have any ceremonies, because without him those big things in my life won't be as meaningful. But I'll take each thing as it comes and who knows what will be going on then.

I think we were lucky that Dad died in his sleep because of heart problems. We didn't know about it ahead of time and I think that G—d helped us with that. If we had known, it would have been awful to have to say good-bye. Like at the beginning, I cried a lot that I just wanted one more kiss or one more minute with him. But then, it would never be enough, and to know the end was coming and then Dad would be gone would be impossible. Really impossible. So if I had to choose, I guess how he died was a good way. But I wish he didn't have to die.

Suggestions

Allie: Everyone has times that are extra sad. That doesn't mean that you're going back to the beginning, when you were crying a whole lot and your eyes were always red and puffy. It just means you're going through a tough stage. Maybe you're stronger and your mind's letting you remember stuff that you didn't remember before. If you cry about it, it means that you're thinking about it and dealing with it. And then you can move on in life, and that's a great thing. If you don't deal with it, it will still be there inside of you, just getting bigger and more in the way. The sadness and grief stuff may be really hard to go through, but it's way harder to not go through it, because then you can't really move on. And in the meantime, you'll be busy getting mad at everyone around you for stupid things because you're so upset and frustrated on the inside.

Being close to your family or friends is very helpful, because you need someone to be supportive and to just listen, and sometimes to help you think things through in a positive way. No matter how awful the situation is, you have to always be thankful that it's not worse. Because it always could be. It could have been a worse death or a million other things. So it's important to keep it in perspective when it all feels like it's the worst thing in the whole world. It's not.

I know there are times when I'm feeling upset and confused and mad and everything else. I don't understand why it happened to *my* dad, to *our* family. I feel like being mean to my sister and brother, and to my mom. And sometimes I am. But it doesn't do any good, and it's really not their fault. I mean, even while I'm being mad I know I'm being ridiculous and it's not their fault. I just feel like I have to take it out on someone. But it's not worth it, because I can always see the sadness in their eyes, and I feel bad for making them sadder.

So I try really hard to find a way to get my bad emotions out, like sadness and anger. I do some relaxation, like meditation. Sometimes I jump rope for ten minutes.

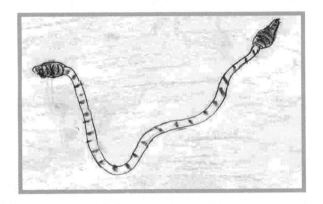

I don't feel like doing it when I start, but I always feel better and calmer when I'm done. At the beginning, it doesn't work that well. But the more you do it, the more you learn to put your bad feelings and mad energy into the jumping, or into whatever. You don't think, *Should I do this?* You just do it without thinking about it. When your time is up, you're pretty much back to feeling normal.

If you know someone who's not dealing with it as well as you are, you should try to help them out if you can because everyone is suffering a loss. Like, my grandma is having a really hard time and cries a lot. I try to be helpful to her, but sometimes it's too much. Her sadness brings me down. At those times, it's better to just get some space. If you can't help the person by being positive or just listening, that's okay. First you need to help yourself, because if you're a mess, you can't help anyone else. But it's not okay to be rude or angry with them if you can help it. But if you can't help it, well, you're just a kid and sometimes you can't help what you do. And it's okay, because that's how it is. Try to find a way to control yourself, apologize if you need to, and move on.

You should always think positively and not negatively. You should realize that you're not the only one this has happened to. Most people have problems of one kind or another, and I bet you're handling yours better than you think. Other people may even have worse problems. Think of the good things you have—your other parent if you still have one, your health, relatives, friends. Some people have a death to deal with and even more extra problems than you do.

We got a lot of sympathy gifts—lots of books, toys, and stuff. And we got to stay home from school. But I would rather go to school and not have such a bad loss. I got straight A's all year and was in the newspaper a couple times. Some kids at school said to me, "Allie, you're so lucky." Can you imagine they would say that? You never realize how lucky you are to have something until it's gone. But if you're reading this, you didn't lose everything. You can think, you have family and friends, and mostly you have life. Focus on the stuff you still have. Feel happy about the good instead of sad about the bad.

David: If you feel sad, remember that you're not the only kid this happens to. And maybe you and your parent can find a grief group to meet other kids who have lost a parent. Hospices usually have those groups. It helps to meet other kids who understand. Even if you don't like them, at least you know you're not alone. The one we tried wasn't quite right for us, so we quit going. You might have to try a few before you find one that's right for you.

It may not seem like it now, but time really does help you get through things. No kids could have loved their dad more than us. He died two years ago and now we're doing pretty well. You get used to your new life. You learn to be glad about what you do have instead of just thinking about what you don't have. I'm happy I had such a great dad, even if it was for too short a time. Some kids have a dad who doesn't really care. Or a dad for a short time who isn't really good. And I'll always have my memories, for my whole life.

Mom has been working a lot more, and that's kind of a bummer. She's trying to work while we're at school and at night, but sometimes she also works in the after-noon. I miss hanging out with her and just doing stuff. I know she has more to do now, but I wish that she had a little more time to just hang out. A lot of things change when a parent dies. The one who's left has more to do and needs to earn more money. So you all have to compromise and have a new schedule. You might not like it, but that's how it is. The best thing to do is be glad about the good stuff.

I'm happy to have two big sisters who I love a lot. I'm happy that my mom is a good one. I'm happy to be healthy. When I'm missing Dad a lot, I try to think about the happy things in my life. Sometimes it doesn't work, so I turn on the TV and get my mind off of it for a while.

Amy: You should talk about your feelings a lot and try to be a team with the rest of your family. Everyone's suffering and everyone is more uptight, so sometimes you and your brothers or sisters or whoever might start fighting. That makes it even harder, because later you feel even worse about it. I think my family has gotten closer because of my dad's death, because we've had to go through so much together. I also know I can rely on them to talk things out with me. Or even if we don't say anything, we're still going through the same stuff, so I know they understand. We all try to be really aware of not blowing up at each other. We're all just trying to be happy and no one needs to be yelled at. If I'm uptight, I try to go somewhere I can be alone. If I'm in the room with the door closed, everyone else knows not to come in. It's important to respect each other's space and privacy. Sometimes it's okay to have a group cry, and other times you just want to be by yourself. I read a book or do an exercise and pretty soon I can feel that I've calmed down.

There are two kinds of people. One kind always cries and never gets over anything. If you're like that, then you're never going to be able to move on. Your life will be worth nothing except tissues. The other kind of person has their down days, but they manage to deal with what comes at them. They try to move on and look at the positives. If you're that kind of person, then you'll be able to have fun and go places you like to go to with your other parent if you have one, or with someone else.

For example, let's say you want to go to Disney World. If you're moving on, then you can go even though it reminds you of the great time that you had when you went with your dad. You may have some hard moments, but you can still do it. And then you feel really great because you did it, and that's what your dad would have wanted for you anyway. If my dad was here, he would've wanted me to be able to move on and not just waste my life crying because I miss him. If I weren't a positive person, I would never even be able to go to Disney World again. Or if I did, I'd have a miserable time crying over what I was missing. Plus, I wouldn't be able to concentrate on my schoolwork and stuff. If Dad were around, he'd say that would be a waste of my life and that I should try to get my act together. And when Dad looks down at me now from heaven, I know he's proud of me for my positive attitude.

I was so close with my dad. We had a really special relationship. Sometimes it feels like he was the only person in the world who really understood me. But other people want to be there for you and understand who you are. You just have to give them a chance.

Allie, Dad, Amy, and David, 11/95

Letters to Dad

Dear Dad,

We had a sleepover at Baba's last night. Amy didn't go because she felt sick. I won an art award and got fifty dollars and now I own a fifty-dollar bill (COOL). I wished you were there to see my art. It was about you and me, so you probably helped me win the first prize.

I wish you were around these days. Cindy's baby, Danny, is already walking. Even though you never met him, he was named after you, so I feel pretty close to him.

We might be moving to Connecticut. I really don't want you to stay down here except it's important for Grammy and Grandpa. And we can always visit with you in our heads so we don't have to go to a cemetery to talk to you. There are only seven days left of school and my teacher was Ms. Cohen this year, who I really liked a lot.

I wish you were here to see my rocket go up in school. It had two parachutes and four wings. And it went up really high and made a lot of smoke. It might have gotten to the very bottom of heaven, but I couldn't really tell from the ground.

I think about you a lot, and everyone says I look a lot like you. That would make me proud except I hope I don't end up with your bald spot. We went to the new Disney park, Animal Kingdom. It was fun, but Mom won't ever go on roller coasters so we really need you around for that.

Love, David

Dear Dad,

I really miss the way we played together more than ever these days because we have been seeing Uncle Andy playing with Danny, and Uncle Steffen playing with the J's. Mom ALMOST got an offer for the house, which means she's probably on the right track. When we were visiting in Connecticut last month, we looked at houses but I really like the ones down here better. Last night, at Grammy and Grandpa's house, we celebrated a holiday. It's always sad without you there. None of us really feel like celebrating, and we don't make as big and fun of a deal out of it as we used to when you were around.

I think I forgot to tell you that Grandpa stopped smoking, but I bet you already know that. This morning the three of us made a play, "The Ballerina Who Couldn't Dance." David was the narrator, Amy was the director and the ballerina who broke her toe, and I was the ballerina who couldn't dance. We messed up a few times, but overall we did wonderful!!

Mom came to school and helped my class make model rockets, and everyone's blasted off great. For David's class, we did one big rocket, an experimental style. He put on two parachutes and extra big wings, and it blasted up SO high, and both parachutes came out perfectly. Tonight we're having Marnie and Nicole sleep over, and we're making up all new rocket styles. One will have fins all the way up, one will be two rockets taped together, and maybe one will be a regular-sized tube with huge fins. We're pretty excited.

When we find out how they do, I'll tell you in my head, even though I know you'll have seen it all. I'll also tell you the rest of my letter in my head, since I'm tired of writing now. I really miss you.

Love always, Allie

Dear Dad,

It still feels like it was just yesterday that you were throwing me in the pool and calling out the crazy names you made up, like the rocket, the paper airplane, the nose cleaner, and the flip. I still can't get it through my head that you're not here.

We just sold our house today. I'm SO psyched about that. I think that you sent us a message, because it's perfect timing. Thank you! The closing date is July 1—wish us happy packing.

I'm attending an award ceremony at school on Thursday. I'll get an award for having my art in a show this year. I'll also get one for being a straight-A student all year, except for handwriting, which I get Bs in. That doesn't count, though.

Lately, we haven't had very many free weekends. Allie and I have been working on floats about Connecticut, because the Parade of States is tomorrow. Everyone in the fourth grade will bring their floats for a one-hour parade around the school. Also, we have to dress up like someone from or someone representing our state. I made Connecticut's state seal on my solid purple T-shirt with permanent markers. My float represents the seasonal changes Connecticut goes through. We even get refreshments and cake afterwards. And—YAHOO—we miss math class! I'll make sure to tap my shoulder tomorrow at the time of the parade.

Will you have to move your spot in heaven to see us better when we move to Connecticut?

I miss you SO much. I love you tons!

Love, Your Ishkabibble—Amy

Looking Back
Five and a Half Years Later

Allie *(now 13 years old):* It's been almost five and a half years now, and I just can't believe how long it's been since Dad was here with us. Just as you accept your religion or nationality as part of your identity, I've learned that family means a lot, too. And in a way, I'm really proud of myself for how I have dealt with Dad's death. I mean, not many people can deal with grief so well, and I'm only a kid.

Almost exactly one year ago I celebrated my *bat mitzvah*, and although all of my family was present, including some relatives I didn't even remember, my own dad was not. Amy and I each held a piece of his *bar mitzvah** speech during our ceremony, and it made us feel like he was with us more. Even though he wasn't there in person, I feel sure that he was the proudest he's been in a long time. I'm sure that in some way he must have been there—if not physically, then definitely in our spirits. It's important to have some kind of belief so that death doesn't seem so final. If I thought that he wasn't still a part of me, I would be much more depressed than I am.

Less than one month ago, Dad's sister got married, which was especially hard for me because Mom's boyfriend was with us. I feel really happy that Mom has found an adult companion to spend time with so maybe when she grows old she won't have to be so alone. Maybe she'll even get married, but we'll think about that when it's time. We're still close to Dad's parents,

*A *bar mitzvah* is the Jewish ceremony that marks a thirteen-year-old boy's transition to adulthood.

although that's been hard. They've had a hard time adjusting to Mom's boyfriend being around, but I know they're trying hard and I know we'll always be close to them. I'm really lonely for Dad still, and I know that's normal and will never fade away. I feel especially sad when there's something meaningful that happens. When everyone is proud of us, I can only guess what Dad would have said since he can't say it himself. Like the idea we had about getting cigarette butts off the beach—it's earned us national awards and international correspondence. Sometimes I think that without a little help from Dad in heaven it wouldn't have gotten this far and that it's kind of a project we're working on together, like we used to.

I still look for signs and talk to him in my head, but the feeling that I have to do that has decreased. Overall, life is better than I ever thought it could be. I have tons of friends, I get good grades, and Mom found a great job that's home based but still involves her law work. I'm especially close to Amy and David, and I have more family near me now. The expression "time will heal everything" is true, but time won't work by itself. You have to have a positive attitude. If you're always negative and never move on, a million years could go by without mending a thing.

Amy (now 13 years old): I can't believe it, but it's been five years since Dad died. At the beginning, I thought my life would never be normal again, even though everyone said time would heal things. Time made things a little better toward the beginning, but it has improved my situation so much now. I feel like a normal kid, not "the kid without a dad."

Mom has a boyfriend now, and he's a very nice man. She's been with him for almost two years. He's nice to our whole family and is a great influence on everyone. Of course, it was difficult to deal with at first. Almost all changes are. But I realized that he wasn't going to take the place of Dad, he was just going to be our companion. Overall, I think that has definitely been a change for the better.

Even after five years, I still have my down times. But I can enjoy the everyday pleasures of life, like laughing, smiling, and just being happy. At first I thought I would never be able to do that.

I still miss Dad a lot, and life has never been and will never be the same without him. There will always be that hole in my heart. Losing a parent isn't something that goes away over time. It will stay with you forever. But there are two ways you can deal with the situation. You can choose not to move on with your life and let your every thought revolve around losing a parent and mourning for them. If you do that, you will never be able to move on with your life and be happy. Or you can also choose to move forward with your life and do things just like you used to. You'll still have sad times, but if you choose to move forward with your life you can have happy times, too.

I've seen people handle the situation both ways. It's easy to stop living your own life and grieve for the person who's dead. But that's not what they would have wanted you to do with your life. Being happy is something that you have to work at. Once you do, you'll know you made the right choice. Don't put your life on hold for someone who would have wanted you to live life to its fullest.

This past summer, I celebrated my *bat mitzvah*. It was a bittersweet day; I was really proud of myself but also sad that Dad wasn't there to celebrate with me. But the sweet overpowered the bitter. I know Dad was watching me and I know how proud he was. When he first passed away, I never thought I'd be able to handle that kind of occasion, but I did and I'm proud of myself for it. You should be proud of yourself for how far you have gotten.

Reflecting on my life so far, it seems to have three parts: life with Dad, life right after Dad died, and life since then. I really feel that losing my dad at such a young age helped me to appreciate life. No one knows what will happen in life—it might just stop suddenly—so you should enjoy every moment. When I look back on how I was when Dad first died, I realize how much I've moved forward. Although initially it may not seem like it, life does move on.

David *(now 9 years old):* It's been five years now and I've come a long way. I don't think about Dad as much as I used to. I'm better at dealing with his death now than when I was four, and now it's not as depressing. We're moving on and now I usually only think about him once or twice a week.

It's still sad, though, when there is a father-son contest, or something like that. Mom has a boyfriend, and it's not as hard as I thought it would be. But no matter how long it's been, or how hard you try, there's always that empty space in your heart that will never get filled in again.

But I think you learn to put the space in its own special part of your heart, and then you still have lots of room for loving and being happy. And that's what Dad would have wanted.

Resources

The Fall of Freddie the Leaf by Leo Buscaglia (New York: Henry Holt and Company, 2002). This simple story about a leaf named Freddie and how he and his companion leaves change with the passing seasons, finally falling to the ground with winter's snow, is an inspiring allegory illustrating the delicate balance between life and death. Ages 4–8.

How It Feels When a Parent Dies by Jill Krementz (New York: Knopf, 1988). Eighteen children from ages 7–17, speak openly of their experiences and feelings. As they speak, readers see them in photos with their surviving parent and with other family members, in the midst of their everyday lives. Children who are experiencing the death of their mother or father will know that they are not alone in their feelings of anger, guilt, anguish, and confusion—that they are even normal. Ages 7 and up.

I Will Remember You: What to Do When Someone You Love Dies: A Guidebook Through Grief for Teens by Laura Dower (New York: Scholastic, 2001). This book encourages young readers to explore the "long, winding tunnel" of the grieving process, to keep going in the face of terrible loss and sadness. It includes personal stories of death and life from real teens, advice from a renowned grief counselor, and dozens of hands-on creative exercises to help teens move through their pain and sorrow. Ages 13 and up.

Sad Isn't Bad: When Someone You Love Dies by Michaelene Mundy (St. Meinrad, IN: One Caring Place/Abbey Press, 1998). Positive, life-affirming advice tells children what they need to know after a loss—the world is still safe; life is good; and hurting hearts do mend. Written by a school counselor, this book helps comfort children facing the worst and hardest kind of reality. Ages 4–8.

What on Earth Do You Do When Someone Dies? by Trevor Romain (Minneapolis: Free Spirit Publishing, 1999). Simple and straight from the heart, this book is for any child who has lost a loved one. The author talks directly to kids about what death means and how to cope. He answers questions kids have about death—Why? What's next? Is it my fault? What's a funeral?—in basic, straightforward terms. Ages 5–10.

When Bad Things Happen to Good People by Harold Kushner (New York: Schocken Books, 2001). Harold Kushner, a Jewish rabbi facing his own child's fatal illness, guides us through the inadequacies of the traditional answers to the problem of evil, then provides practical and compassionate advice on how to cope with tragedy, what to do about anger, and how to keep from feeling guilty. Ages young adult and up.

About the Authors

Allie, David, and Amy Dennison live and attend school outside of New Haven, Connecticut. They have won several awards for their environmental endeavors and their "No Butts About It" campaign. They received a Presidential Environmental Youth Award, were named Millennium Dreamers for Disney, and were given a Keep Florida Beautiful Award for Outstanding Personal Achievement. In addition, Amy, Allie, and David have presented their campaign to hundreds of people and have spoken with U.S. Congresspeople, State Senators, heads of environmental and governmental agencies, and all sorts of people in between.

After the September 11 tragedies, the Dennisons donated stapled-together versions of their journal book to various charities so it would be available to child victims of the attacks.

Other Great Books from Free Spirit

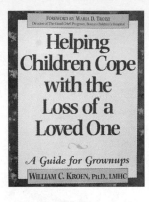

Helping Children Cope with the Loss of a Loved One
A Guide for Grownups
by William C. Kroen, Ph.D., LMHC
This book explains how children from infancy through age 18 perceive and react to death. It also suggests ways to respond to children at different ages and stages, and describes specific strategies for guiding and supporting them through the grieving process. For parents and educators.
$14.95; 112 pp.; softcover; 7¼" x 9¼"

When A Friend Dies
A Book for Teens About Grieving and Healing
by Marilyn E. Gootman, Ed.D.
Marilyn Gootman offers genuine understanding and gentle advice for any grieving teen. She knows what teenagers go through when another teen dies; she has seen her own children suffer from the death of a friend. She has written this book out of compassion, love, and a genuine desire to help young people cope and heal. For ages 11 & up.
$9.95; 120 pp.; softcover; 5" x 7"

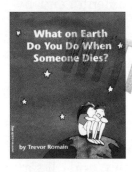

What on Earth Do You Do When Someone Dies?
Written and illustrated by Trevor Romain
Simple, insightful, and straight from the heart, this book is for any child who has lost a loved one or other special person. For ages 5–10.
$7.95; 72 pp.; softcover; illust.; 5⅛" x 6"

"The concise, truthful answers and drawings will comfort children who are coping with the death of a loved one." —*Library Talk*

To place an order or to request a free catalog of SELF-HELP FOR KIDS® and SELF-HELP FOR TEENS® materials, please write, call, email, or visit our Web site:

Free Spirit Publishing Inc. • 217 Fifth Avenue North • Suite 200 Minneapolis, MN 55401-1299 • toll-free 800.735.7323 • local 612.338.2068 fax 612.337.5050 • help4kids@freespirit.com

Visit our online catalog at www.freespirit.com